THE COMPLETE MINISTRY AUDIT

THE COMPLETE MINISTRY AUDIT

SECOND EDITION

BILL EASUM
With Robert Brydia

ABINGDON PRESS / Nashville

THE COMPLETE MINISTRY AUDIT
SECOND EDITION

Copyright © 2006 by Abingdon Press

This book is printed on acid-free paper.

Library of Congress Cataloging-in-Publication Data

Easum, William M., 1939-
    The complete ministry audit.—2nd ed. / Bill Easum with Robert Brydia.
    p. cm.
    ISBN 0-687-49750-7 (binding: pbk. w/cd insert : alk. paper)
    1. Church growth. 2. Church growth—Evaluation. I. Brydia, Robert. II. Title.

BV652.25.E28 2006
254—dc 22

2005026975

06 07 08 09 10 11 12 13 14 15—10 9 8 7 6 5 4 3 2 1
MANUFACTURED IN THE UNITED STATES OF AMERICA

CONTENTS

The Top Ten Reasons for Using *The Complete Ministry Audit* 2.0

10. Many church leaders say it is the most comprehensive tool available.

9. You don't have to leave home to do it.

8. Laity are personally involved in the process of arriving at the actual recommendations.

7. *The Complete Ministry Audit* provides you a proven step-by-step process for developing disciples.

6. *The Complete Ministry Audit* provides you the tools you need in order to think and act strategically about your congregation and its mission.

5. You can save thousands of dollars by not having Bill Easum or one of his team come to your church for an on-site consultation.

4. You have a CD-ROM containing spreadsheet files to make data collection easier.

3. Once you purchase this workbook, you have permission to copy all of the data-collection forms for distribution throughout your congregation (but no other congregation).

2. You have at your fingertips the knowledge that Bill Easum has gained from more than five hundred local church consultations.

1. It works in both traditional and nontraditional churches!

We encourage you to use the bonus CD-ROM to do all of your data compiling, averaging, and printing reports.

SECTION ONE

GETTING STARTED

Don't Begin Without Reading This Section!

The Complete Ministry Audit, Second Edition, is designed to help traditional *and* nontraditional congregations thrive in the twenty-first century. The process you are about to begin is more a diagnosis than an evaluation. The team leading this process will function like physicians. Physicians diagnose and prescribe. They do not make judgments. Sometimes the prescription is a remedy, sometimes it is preventative medicine, and sometimes it is radical surgery. But never is the prescription a value judgment about the person involved. The same is true about the Ministry Audit. It is a diagnosis meant to help, not judge. The process ends with concrete recommendations that will help your church thrive in the emerging world.

Expect to take a minimum of five to six weeks to complete the process. As you go through the process, look for patterns that jump out at you. Don't get lost in the detail. *Unfreezing Moves,* by Bill Easum (published by Abingdon Press), will help you in the process, although it is not required.

To make the process work smoothly, think of two broad actions you must take:

- One, collect and fill out all of the data asked for in the Surveys and the Worship Survey;
- Two, transfer that same data into the Ministry Audit in section 4. Every survey must be entered into its proper place within *The Complete Ministry Audit.*

It's that simple. So, let's get started!

Step One: Overview of the Material

The Compete Ministry Audit includes the following key documents. Leaving out any one of them will leave gaps in the audit.

- Staff Survey (D:\Surveys\Staff\Staff.doc)
- The Readiness Survey for Staff (D:\Surveys\Staff\Staff-Readiness.doc)
- The Permission Giving Survey for Staff (D:\Surveys\Staff\Staff-Permission.doc)
- Official Body Survey (D:\Surveys\Body\Body.doc)
- The Official Body Readiness Survey (D:\Surveys\Body\Body-Readiness.doc)
- The Permission Giving Survey for Official Body (D:\Surveys\Body\Body-Permission.doc)
- The Worship Survey to be filled out on four consecutive Sundays by those worshipping (or on any other days worship occurs) (D:\Surveys\Worship\Worship-Week1.doc through Worship-Week4.doc)

All of these documents are to be collated and averaged and placed into the final document—*The Complete Ministry Audit.*

Suggestion: Using the files on the CD-ROM will make your task much easier and more productive. The following files on the CD-ROM will help you to record and collate your survey results.

- The Body Survey Totals Spreadsheet (D:\Spreadsheets\Body Survey-Totals Spreadsheet.xls)
- The Readiness Totals Spreadsheet (D:\Spreadsheets\Readiness Survey-Totals Spreadsheet.xls)
- The Permission Giving Totals Spreadsheet (D:\Spreadsheets\Permission Giving Survey-Totals Spreadsheet.xls)
- The Worship Survey Totals Spreadsheet (D:\Spreadsheets\Worship Survey-Totals Spreadsheet.xls)

Note that there is no spreadsheet with which to compile the staff survey data, as it is mostly informational, both current and historical.

The CD-ROM also contains a file for every survey that you need to use as part of your audit.

Step Two: Select a Steering Team

We've found that it is helpful to establish a steering team of seven people, including the lead pastor, to oversee the process from start to finish. Your team will be responsible for collecting the data, and if you are doing the audit by yourself, your team will also be analyzing the data, arriving at recommendations, sharing your recommendations with the congregation, shepherding prudent action, and securing any necessary resources to aid in the process. A lengthy list of regularly updated resources is provided at www.easumbandy.com; click Free Resources, then FAQs.

If you are doing this process either by mail or in preparation for Bill Easum to do an on-site consultation with your church, then the steering team will only be responsible for collecting the data and then shepherding the action on the recommendations from Bill Easum.

Suggestion: Even though you may use a steering team, we've found it is best when the steering team appoints one person to oversee the collection of data from the official body and one person to oversee the collection of data from the staff and the Worship Survey. Also, we have found that the process goes much more smoothly and quickly if one person is responsible for the entry of the statistical data into the Ministry Audit. This person needs to have a computer that runs Microsoft Windows 98 and Excel 97 or higher. If the church has an administrator, ask that person to do all of the statistical work.

Step Three: Begin the Worship Survey

We suggest that you begin the Worship Survey as early in the process of diagnosis as possible since you need four weeks to conduct it. You should also begin collecting the data while taking the survey. Make enough copies of the Worship Survey (pages

15-16, or print from the disk the following files: D:\Surveys\Worship\Worship-Week 1-4.doc; from this point on we will assume that the drive letter of your CD-ROM drive is "D") to distribute to each adult who attends worship over the four-week period. After all of the surveys have been completed, calculate the averages and turn to section 4 of this workbook and record those averages in the Ministry Audit or use the spreadsheet on the bonus CD-ROM, which does all of the calculations for you. The information from the Worship Survey is used in several places—be sure to tabulate and enter it in the appropriate places in the Ministry Audit.

If you use the spreadsheet file "D:\Spreadsheets\Worship Survey-Totals Spreadsheet.xls," simply enter the numbers into each cell, and the spreadsheet formulas will do the calculations for you, so that a report can later be printed and the numbers inserted in the master audit.

Some parishioners may ask the following question about the Worship Survey: "Do I really have to fill it out all four Sundays?" The answer is simple. People are asked to fill it out every Sunday they attend because we want to get an accurate picture of what attendance looks like on an average Sunday. Some people attend every Sunday and some people are more sporadic. The responses of those who attend every Sunday should receive more weight than someone who is there just one Sunday out of the four. This is called a "weighted" average.

Step Four: Order the Percept Demographic Map

Order a Percept Demographic Report. All you need is the Map. You don't need the Compass. To order a copy call 800-442-6277, or visit www.perceptnet.com. While this material is not covered or included in *The Complete Ministry Audit,* it provides valuable information about your surrounding community. If you are doing *The Complete Ministry Audit* yourself but would like someone else to interpret the data, I will be happy to do it for you. Just call our office at 361-749-5364 or e-mail us at Easum@easumbandy.com. If you are preparing the Ministry Audit for an on-site consultation with me, then the demographic interpretation is included in the consultation, if you provide the Percept Report. (Note: Some denominations offer a diluted version to their churches for free. That material will not offer you the kind of help you really need. If you are including the demographics with an on-site consultation, please order the complete Map from Percept.)

Step Five: Collect Information

Give copies of the Staff Surveys (pages 17-39 below, or print out the following files: D:\Surveys\Staff\Staff.doc; D:\Surveys\Staff\Staff-Permission.doc; and D:\Surveys\ Staff\Staff-Readiness.doc) to each person who is a paid member of your staff. When each staff person finishes answering the questions, the collated answers are to be recorded in the Ministry Audit in section 4 or in the spreadsheets on the CD-ROM under the file names:

- The Readiness Totals Spreadsheet (D:\Spreadsheets\Readiness Survey-Totals Spreadsheet.xls)
- The Permission Giving Totals Spreadsheet (D:\Spreadsheets\Permission Giving Survey-Totals Spreadsheet.xls)

The questions included in the staff survey are primarily informational data, both historical and current. Collate (average) the answers on a separate Staff Survey and *use that copy to complete the Ministry Audit by transferring the results to the Ministry Audit itself in section 4.*

> The Staff Surveys can be found on pages 17-39 below.
> The corresponding survey files on the CD-ROM are "D:\Surveys\Staff\Staff.doc" (Staff Survey), "D:\Surveys\Staff\Staff-Readiness.doc" (Staff Readiness Survey), and "D:\Surveys\Staff\Staff-Permission.doc" (Staff Permission Giving Survey).

- Decide how you are going to gather information that is asked for in the Official Body Survey. (The official body of your church is the church board, the administrative board, the elders, the session, or however you designate the body of church officials.) Some churches collect the information at a meeting of the official body (best option); others mail it to the official body.
- Give a copy of the Official Body Survey to each member of your official body to complete. You can copy the printed version on pages 39-43 or you can use the electronic version on the disk (D:\Surveys\Body\Body.doc.).
- Collate (average) the answers on a separate Official Body Survey and *use that copy to complete the Ministry Audit by transferring the results to the Ministry Audit itself in section 4.* (Because of the one to ten scaling factor on these worksheets, the answer will be a number arrived at by averaging the responses. Do not use "yes" or "no.") Insert the average into the proper places in the Ministry Audit. The questions in the audit marked with an asterisk are those taken from the Official Body Survey. Hint: Use the file "D:\Spreadsheets\Body Survey-Totals Spreadsheet.xls" on the CD-ROM to ease the workload of compiling the Official Body Surveys.

> The Official Body Survey can be found on pages 39-43.
> The corresponding files on the CD-ROM are "D:\Surveys\Body\Body.doc" (Official Body Survey), "D:\Surveys\Body\Body-Readiness.doc" (Official Body Readiness Survey), and "D:\Surveys\Body\Body-Permission.doc" (Official Body Permission Giving Survey).

Step Six: Transfer All Survey Data to the Complete Ministry Audit

Once all the surveys from the staff and official body are answered, transfer the data to the Complete Ministry Audit in section 4. This task will make more sense if the person compiling the Complete Ministry Audit has read this section.

Understanding the Complete Ministry Audit

The information in the Complete Ministry Audit is about your church and not about your community.

Two Types of Questions

Type One Questions. The numbers with an asterisk are subjective questions that have no right or wrong answers. These questions deal with how people perceive their church and its leadership. They are answered from one to ten with one indicating total agreement with the question and ten indicating total disagreement. A response of five often indicates that the respondent did not have a strong opinion about the question. Any response below four is a positive, and any response above six is a negative. In other words, the lower the score the more positive the perception is to the growth of your church and the people. (There are two questions that are exceptions and require a high response, but you will know these when you see them.) These questions were answered by the official administrative body of your church. I have supplied the average scores for all of the questions with an asterisk. These averages come from the scores of more than 250 churches throughout the United States. If yours is a Canadian church, add .30 to all of the answers. Any score that is more than .50 above or below the average score is outside of the norm for that answer either positively or negatively. For example, if the average score provided is 3.56 and your score is 4.22, it is outside the norm to the negative and could indicate a weakness that needs to be addressed. If the average score is 3.05 and your score is 3.35, you are within the norm. If the average score is 3.10 and your score is 2.2, you are outside the norm to the positive. Such a score is excellent and is what you hope to see in many of the scores. How the scores compare to hundreds of other churches is what gives them positive or negative values. A high score does not mean your church is bad. It simply means that you may need to look more closely at the factors that pushed you outside the norm.

In most cases it is wise to look at the overall patterns that emerge instead of looking at the individual scores. However, some of the questions merit special attention. The crucial ones are noted and explained in the study guide in section 2. You will do well to analyze the collated answers carefully. In some cases you may want to look at the scores of each respondent. (You can do that without knowing the respondent's identity because respondents do not put their names on any of the surveys.) You might want to review the surveys if your averages are too high and you didn't have a lot of respondents fill out the surveys. Sometimes you will see one or two of the respondents ruining the scores because their answers were consistently high. When you find this to be the case you know approximately how many control freaks or unhappy people make up your leadership.

When the numbers are tabulated, ask yourself, "Do the overall scores suggest a pattern?" Keep in mind that the lower the scores, the healthier the church.

Type Two Questions. The statements without an asterisk deal with fact more than perception and are compiled from the various records in the church and the survey taken in worship.

Traditional and Nontraditional

Throughout the Ministry Audit, I refer to traditional and nontraditional churches. Traditional churches rely primarily on Sunday school, have worship primarily on Sunday, use traditional liturgical forms of worship, do not stress small groups in homes, and do not use contemporary forms of worship. Nontraditional churches stress small groups in homes, practice contemporary forms of worship, may have more than one location, and may not stress or have adult Sunday school.

Decide which type of church you are: traditional, nontraditional, moving from traditional to nontraditional, or moving from nontraditional to traditional. Many of the actions you will need to take in response to the Ministry Audit depend on which one of these categories best describes your congregation.

19 Growth Principles

The Ministry Audit is organized around nineteen growth principles. Not all of these growth principles are important to every church. Some will be important to your church and some will not. It depends on your church's stage of development. You should know which ones apply to your church when you complete the Ministry Audit.

Key Questions

As you analyze the audit, you will notice that not all of the questions in the Ministry Audit are addressed in the study guide (section 5). What I have tried to do is focus on the questions that are most often crucial to strategic thinking as well as those that require some explanation. These questions are listed and explained in the study guide. Knowing how the church addresses these questions is essential to any type of strategic thinking.

Approach the Ministry Audit as if it were a puzzle, which means that you have to put the pieces together to see what the picture looks like. So, wait until all of the pieces of the audit are in place before you jump to any conclusions.

Don't get lost in the details of the completed picture. Look at the big picture. The primary mistake leaders make when doing the process is getting lost in the details long before they map out any action plans.

It's Time to Start the Process!

It's time now to put together the puzzle.

Suggestion: Keep the following page handy at all times. Doing so will save lots of headaches along the way.

Ministry Audit Preparation Checklist

Date Completed	
	Carefully review all instructions, Surveys, and Spreadsheets. We encourage you to use the files on the CD-ROM.
	Even though you may use a steering team, assign *one person* to oversee the completion of information gathering.
	Prepare Worship Surveys to be completed by the congregation for four consecutive weeks. Week One ☐ Week Two ☐ Week Three ☐ Week Four ☐
	Give each staff member a copy of the Staff Survey and have each person complete the section that applies to his or her area of responsibility. Hint: The Staff Survey is located on the CD-ROM at "D:\Surveys\Staff\Staff.doc."
	Make sure each program staff member completes the Readiness Survey and the Permission Giving Survey. Hint: The Staff Permission Giving Survey is located on the CD-ROM at "D:\Surveys\Staff\Staff-Permisson.doc." The Staff Readiness Survey is located on the CD-ROM at "D:\Surveys\Staff\Staff-Readiness.doc."
	Mail (or give out at the meeting) copies of the Official Body Survey and the Permission Giving and Readiness surveys to each member of the official body to complete. Request that they be returned as soon as possible, and point out the need to complete all questions. Hint: The Official Body Survey is located on the CD-ROM at "D:\Surveys\Body\Body.doc." The Body Permission Giving Survey is located on the CD-ROM at "D:\Surveys\Body\Body-Permisson.doc." The Body Readiness Survey is located on the CD-ROM at "D:\Surveys\Body\Body-Readiness.doc."
	All copies of Staff Surveys received and compiled.
	All copies of Body Surveys received and compiled.
	Information from Staff Surveys entered into working copy of the Ministry Audit.
	Information from Official Body Surveys entered into working copy of the Ministry Audit. Put the actual numbers, not Yes or No. Hint: Use the file "D:\Spreadsheets\Body Survey-Totals Spreadsheet.xls" on the CD-ROM.
	Make sure both staff *and* the official body have completed the Readiness Survey and that the averages of responses are listed on the appropriate Readiness Totals Sheet. Hint: Use the file "D:\Spreadsheets\Readiness Survey-Totals Spreadsheet.xls" on the CD-ROM.
	Make sure both staff *and* the official body have completed the Permission Giving Survey and that the averages of responses are listed on the appropriate Readiness Totals Sheet. Hint: Use the file "D:\Spreadsheets\Permission Giving Survey-Totals Spreadsheet.xls" on the CD-ROM.
	Either give the completed Ministry Audit to the appropriate group in your church to analyze and report to the congregation or send it to Bill Easum for analysis.
	Give each participant a copy of the completed Ministry Audit.
Remember: The number one mistake people make in this process is not transferring all of the data to the actual Ministry Audit.	

Section Two

Surveys

This section contains the surveys that you will use to prepare the audit. The Complete Ministry Audit, however, is in section 4. Before you complete the actual audit, either photocopy the audit for use in subsequent years or use the Growth Principle Templates on the CD-ROM (preferred method) (files D:\Growth Principles\Growth Principle 1 – 19.doc). Many churches have found it helpful to conduct portions of the Ministry Audit on an annual basis.

Several files are supplied on the CD-ROM in spreadsheet form for your use to help with the surveys. You will need a computer running Microsoft Windows 98 and Excel 97 or higher. The file names are in parentheses below. See appendix 2 for complete instructions on how to use the files on the CD-ROM.

The surveys are as follows:

Worship Survey (D:\Surveys\Worship-Week 1.doc through D:\Surveys\Worship-Week 4.doc)

Staff Survey (D:\Surveys\Staff\Staff.doc)

Staff Readiness Survey (D:\Surveys\Staff\Staff-Readiness.doc)

Staff Permission Giving Survey (D:\Surveys\Staff\Staff-Permission.doc)

Official Body Survey (D:\Surveys\Body\Body.doc)

Official Body Readiness Survey (D:\Surveys\Body\Body-Readiness.doc)

Official Body Permission Giving Survey (D:\Surveys\Body\Body-Permission.doc)

Survey Form for Worship

(D:\Surveys\Worship-Week 1.doc through D:\Surveys\Worship-Week 4.doc on the CD-ROM)

1. I was born between:
   1900 and 1924_____
   1925 and 1945_____
   1946 and 1964_____
   1965 and 1984_____
   After 1984_____

2. My gender is:
   Male _____
   Female _____

3. My marital status is:
   Married _____
   Single _____

4. The number of people in my car this morning was _____.

5. The number of miles I drive or commute to church is:
   Less than one ____
   One to three ____
   Four to six ____
   Seven to ten ____
   Eleven to fifteen ____
   More than fifteen ____

6. In relation to the church, my home is in what direction?
   N___   NE___   E___   SE___   S___   SW___   W ___   or NW___

7. The number of miles I drive or commute to work is _____.

8. The number of minutes I drive or commute to work is _____.

9. What music do I listen to the most?
   Country ___
   Jazz ___
   Classical ___
   Christian ___
   Hard Rock ___
   Soft Rock ___
   East Listening ___
   1950–60s Music ___
   News/Talk ___
   National Public Radio ___
   Rap ___

10. I am a
    New Visitor ___
    Continuing Visitor ___
    Member ___
    I usually attend the _____ worship service.

11. Our yearly household income is
    Less than $7,500 ___
    $7,500 to $14,999 ___
    $15,000 to $24,999 ___
    $25,000 to $34,999 ___
    $35,000 to $49,999 ___
    $50,000 to $74,999 ___
    $75,000 to $99,999 ___
    $100,000 to $124,999 ___
    $125,000 or more ___

12. Are you currently in a small group at the church (fifteen people or fewer)?

Yes _____

No _____

13. Are you currently serving in some capacity?

Yes _____

No _____

14. Do you have access to electronic mail?

Yes _____

No _____

Staff Survey

(D:\Surveys\Staff\Staff.doc on the CD-ROM)

CHURCH: _____

DATE: _____

Questions 1, 95, 109, 110, and 111 are Worship Survey questions. Please conduct a written survey in worship for four Sundays to obtain this information. (See separate Survey Form.) Ask each person in worship to fill out the survey each week. (Try to avoid scheduling this survey during holidays.)

Note: Please mark "confidential" on any answers you do not wish to be shared with your congregation.

Growth Principle 1

1. What is the age, gender, and marital status of adult worshippers? (from the Worship Survey)

(M/M = male/married; M/S = male/single; F/M = female/married; F/S = female/single)

Born between 1900 and 1924	Born between 1925 and 1945	Born between 1946 and 1964	Born between 1965 and 1984	Born after 1984		
No.: ____	No.: ____	No.: ____	No.: ____	No.: ____		
%: ____	%: ____	%: ____	%: ____	%: ____		
M/M ____	M/M ____	M/M ____	M/M ____	M/M ____	Male: ____	% ____
M/S ____	M/S ____	M/S ____	M/S ____	M/S ____	Female: ____	% ____
F/M ____	F/M ____	F/M ____	F/M ____	F/M ____	Married: ____	% ____
F/S ____	F/S ____	F/S ____	F/S ____	F/S ____	Single: ____	% ____

What are the population statistics (broken down by age) for our area? (Contact the Chamber of Commerce for this information if your church did not order Percept.)

Percentage Born Between:

1900 and 1924_____% 1925 and 1945_____% 1946 and 1964_____% 1965 and 1984_____%
After 1984_____%

2. What are our people programs, including specialized ministries?

_____
_____
_____
_____

3. Has there been any major controversy or division in the last five years?

_____
_____
_____
_____

4. What is our decision-making process?

_____
_____
_____
_____

5. Who gives or withholds permission for new ideas or ministries in our church?

_____
_____
_____
_____

6. What is our church known for on the community grapevine?

_____
_____
_____
_____

7. Describe our local church organizational structure.

_____
_____
_____
_____

Growth Principle 2

8. Does our church offer a balanced ministry? _____

List the various programs under the following headings:

Love (Nurture)	Justice (Social Action)	Mercy (Evangelism)
_____	_____	_____
_____	_____	_____
_____	_____	_____
_____	_____	_____
_____	_____	_____

9. Does our church have a preschool? _____
   How many attend? _____

10. Does our church have a grade school? _____
    How many attend? _____

11. Does our church have a parent's day out program? _____
    How many attend? _____

12. Does our church have a day care? _____
    How many attend? _____

13. Does our church have adult day care? _____
    How many attend? _____

14. Do we start a new Sunday school class every three to six months? _____

15. Number of adult Sunday school classes: _____
    How many attend? _____

16. Number of singles' Sunday school classes: _____
    How many attend? _____

17. Number of youth Sunday school classes: _____
    How many attend? _____

18. Number of children's Sunday school classes: _____
    How many attend? _____

19. When was the newest adult Sunday school class started? _____

20. List Sunday evening programs and approximate attendance:

    _____

    _____

21. List midweek programs and approximate attendance:

    _____

    _____

22. List Bible studies and approximate attendance:

_____
_____
_____

23. List athletic programs:

_____
_____
_____

24. Does our church have a mentoring program? If so, describe:

_____
_____
_____

25. List other programs:

_____
_____
_____

Growth Principle 3

26. What is our nominating process?

_____
_____
_____

27. Do we encourage and use spiritual gifts inventories? _____
    If so, describe the material and the process:

_____
_____
_____

Growth Principle 4

28. List the membership figures for the last ten years, with the most recent year first.

Year	Membership

29. List our membership losses for the last ten years, with the most recent year first.

Year	Death	Withdrawal	Transfer to Same Denomination	Transfer to Other Denomination	Total

30. Do we concentrate on assimilating new members within the first three months? _____

31. Is a staff person or volunteer responsible for the assimilation of new members? _____

32. Does our church have enough small groups for the size of our church? _____
    (You need one small group for every ten people in worship.)
    To determine this number:
    a. Divide worship attendance by ten; _____
    b. Count the number of small groups with fifteen or fewer in attendance (include Sunday school classes); _____
    c. Subtract line a from line b to determine the number over or under what is needed. _____

33. List the number of each of the following small groups (do not count Sunday school classes):
    a. Recovery _____
    b. Support _____
    c. Learning _____
    d. Mission or Discipling _____
    e. Institutional (required denominational) _____

34. What percent of the congregation is inactive? _____

35. Have we cleaned our rolls within the last three years? _____

36. Describe our assimilation program:

_____

_____

_____

_____

Growth Principle 5

37. List the amount of money given to all causes outside our congregation for the past ten years.

(List most recent year first and include all denominational and judicatory support, i.e., apportionments.)

Year	Amount Given

Growth Principle 7 (No questions for Principle 6)

38. On how many Sundays per year does our lead pastor preach? _____

39. Do we regularly have different pastors preach or do we have more than one pastor preach each week? _____

40. How many Sundays a year does the service contain a sermon? _____

41. How many Sundays a year is there a sermon from our associate pastor? _____

42. List the size of our present adult and youth choir(s) and at which service they sing.

Choir	Service	Present Size	Ideal Size*

To determine the ideal size for each choir for each service, divide the attendance for each service at which the choir sings by ten.

Copyright © 2006 by Abingdon Press. Reproduced with permission.

43. What is the percentage of worship attendance to membership? _____

44. Do we have an attendance tracking system? _____
    Do we use it? _____
    If so, how?

    _____

    _____

    _____

45. Analyze the worship growth pattern for the last ten years. List the most current year first.

Year	Average Attendance			Total	Percent Increase (+) or Decrease (-)
	Service 1	Service 2	Service 3		

Worship has increased/decreased _____% in the last ten years.

(Determine percentage of growth each year. For example, take the amount of difference between years one and two and divide it by year one.)

46. Do we use multimedia in our worship on a weekly basis? _____

Growth Principle 8

47. How many Sunday morning worship services do we offer? _____
    What are the hours? _____   _____   _____

48. Average attendance at each: _____   _____   _____

49. Do we have worship at any other time of the week? _____
    If so, when? _____

50. Do we have any satellite services? _____
    If so, how do we accomplish them?

    _____

    _____

    _____

51. If offering more than one service, does the same pastor preach each service, or is there a choice of speakers? _____
    If using more than one speaker, please describe:

    _____

    _____

    _____

52. Are we willing to have a worship service at the same time we have Sunday school? _____

53. When was the newest service started? _____
    Which one was it? _____

54. Does each service have a regular choir or band? _____
    If not, which ones do not?

    _____

    _____

    _____

55. Is there a youth choir that sings regularly? _____

56. How many Sundays a year does our major adult choir sing? _____

57. Does our major adult choir take a vacation? _____

58. How many children's choirs does our church have? _____
    How often do they sing? _____

59. How many Christmas Eve services does our church have? _____
    Describe each service, and list the hours that each service is offered:

    _____

    _____

    _____

    _____

Growth Principle 9

60. List all senior pastors, with dates of service, for the past twenty years: _____

    _____

    _____

    _____

61. Tenure of present lead pastor: _____

62. How much vacation do our pastors and staff receive?

    _____

    _____

    _____

Growth Principle 10

63. List all current *paid* staff, giving name, job title, salary, length of service, and whether they are full- or part-time. (Add up program staff and support staff not by the actual number of people but by how the total equates to full-time positions. For example, two half-time people equal one full-time person. See Principle 10, question 2.) Attach this list to the Complete Ministry Audit when you make the final transfer.

_____

_____

_____

_____

_____

_____

_____

_____

64. Has the number of staff kept pace with the growth of the church? _____

65. Are we staffed for *Decline, Maintenance,* or *Growth* based on the answer to question 63? _____

66. Is the role of our associate pastor that of apprentice, professional, or retired? _____

67. Is there adequate continuing education money in the budget for each paid staff member? _____

68. Does our paid staff hold weekly staff meetings? _____
    If so, on a separate piece of paper, describe a typical staff meeting and attach this list to the Complete Ministry Audit.

69. Does each paid staff member have an opportunity to have input into the staff agenda? _____

70. Are new ideas welcome at the staff meetings from the paid staff? _____

71. Does the paid staff have yearly retreats? _____

72. Does the paid staff gather on Sunday mornings to make sure all bases are covered? _____

73. What percent of our budget do our salaries represent? _____

74. Is there a certain time each week set aside by the lead pastor during which individual paid staff members can make appointments to consult with the pastor? _____

75. Does the lead pastor share his or her vision for the congregation at the staff meetings? _____

76. Has our staff had formal training in time management? _____

Growth Principle 11

77. Use the following chart to determine the actual size of our church in relation to other Protestant churches.

Average Worship Attendance	Larger Than What Percent of Churches
1-49	40.5
50-74	57.5
75-99	69.1
100-149	81.6
150-199	88.6
200-349	96.3
350-499	98.4
500-749	99.3
750-999	99.6
1000+	99.7

Based on these figures, our church is larger than _____% of all Protestant churches. (These figures may vary a few percentage points from denomination to denomination.)

78. Is our leadership's perception of our church's size the same as the reality of our church's size? _____

79. What is our greatest challenge in developing lay leaders? Recruiting? Equipping? Identifying? Deploying? _____

80. How do we raise up leaders?

_____

_____

_____

Growth Principle 12

81. In the past, has our church missed any "windows of opportunity"? _____
   If so, what were they?

_____

_____

_____

82. Do we need more worship space? _____
   (Do not estimate or rely solely on an architect's estimate. Measure the capacity of your sanctuary by actually counting how many people can sit on a pew comfortably, and then compute a total by

multiplying this number by the number of pews throughout the sanctuary. Another option is to measure actual pew length and divide by twenty-two inches.)

  a. Sanctuary capacity: _____
  b. Eighty percent of capacity: _____
  c. Average attendance at largest service: _____
     (If c is larger than b, you need more worship space.)

83. Is our worship capacity more than 50 percent larger than our Sunday school capacity? (Compare line 82a, above, with line 86b, below.) _____

84. Do we need more choir space? _____
  a. Choir space capacity: _____
  b. Eighty percent of capacity: _____
  c. Average main attendance: _____
     (If line c is larger than line b, you need more choir space.)

85. Do we need more nursery space? _____
  a. Nursery capacity: _____
  b. Eighty percent of capacity: _____
  c. Average main attendance: _____
     (If line c is larger than line b, you need more nursery space.)

  How many nursery personnel are on duty for the largest worship service? _____
  Is there a nursery available for all events? _____
  Are infants and toddlers separated? _____
  Are there any written nursery policies that are given to the parents? _____
  Do we have adequate security in place to avoid noncustodial kidnapping? _____
  Is the nursery close to the sanctuary and on the same floor? _____
  Do we offer pagers to first-time users of our nursery? _____

86. Do we need more education space? _____
  Allow thirty square feet per person for students kindergarten age and younger; twenty square feet per person for those in first grade or above. Draw a floor plan for each level of each building and show the capacity of each room and the average attendance of the class. From this figure, calculate the education capacity.
  a. Education capacity: _____
  b. Eighty percent of capacity: _____
  c. Average main attendance: _____
     (If line c is larger than line b, you need more education space.)

87. Is each one of our Sunday school classes at less than 80 percent of the capacity for its space? _____

88. Which classes are at greater than 80 percent of capacity?

  _____

  _____

  _____

  Do we need to rearrange any of these classes? _____

89.   Number of classrooms available: _____
        Number of classrooms presently used: _____

90. List the total Sunday school average attendance and percent of growth for each of the last ten years (most recent year first):

Year	Average Attendance	Percent Increase (+) or Decrease (-)

Sunday school has increased/decreased _____ percent in the last ten years.

91. Do we have more than one session of Sunday school? _____
    If so, please list times and attendance of each:

    _____

    _____

    _____

92. According to the 80 percent rule, does our church need to add space? _____
    If so, where?

    _____

    _____

    _____

Growth Principle 13

93. Does our church own enough land? _____
    If we currently own fewer than ten acres, is there adjacent property for sale? _____
    We own: _____
    We need: _____

94. What is the average attendance of the largest worship service? _____
    If Sunday school and worship occur at the same hour, count the total number in attendance at that hour if this combined total is larger than other worship service attendance.

95. Average number of people per car (from Worship Survey, question 4): _____

96. Number of paved off-street parking spaces available (please count): _____

97. Eighty percent of this number of parking spaces is (multiply line 96 by 0.80): _____

98. Number of spaces needed to accommodate attendance (divide line 95 into line 94): _____

99. How many spaces do we need to add? _____
    If line 98 is larger than line 97, more spaces are needed. If line 97 is larger than line 98, no more spaces are needed. (Remember: This is an immediate need and does not consider future growth.)

Growth Principle 14

100. If we plan or need to build, how much is the approximate yearly debt service on the new facility we will need to build? _____

101. What percent of our budget would this be? _____

102. a. Our total indebtedness is: _____
     b. The percent of our present debt service to our budget is (see Growth Principle 17, question 24): _____

103. The percent of our debt service to budget with a new facility added will be (line 100 + line 102b): _____

104. When was the last building program? _____

105. What was built?

     _____

     _____

     _____

Growth Principle 15

106. Breakdown of new members for the past ten years (list most recent year first):

Year	Profession of Faith	Other Denomination	Same Denomination	Total
TOTALS:				

107. Does column one outnumber columns two and three? _____

108. Do we intentionally reach out to the unchurched? _____
     If yes, describe how on a separate piece of paper.

109. What is the average number of miles our members drive to work? (Worship Survey, question 7)
     _____

110. What is the average number of minutes our members drive to work? (Worship Survey, question 8)
     _____

111. What is the average number of miles our members drive to church? (Worship Survey, question 5)
     _____

     (If the answer to question 109 is larger than the answer to question 111, concentrate on meeting the needs of the people represented in those miles.)

     Answers to questions 112, 113, 115, and 117 can be obtained through your Chamber of Commerce or Percept. However, we strongly suggest that you obtain a Percept Demographic Study of your area. We recommend you order only the Map and the free transparencies of your choice. If you supply the Percept Demographic study with the Ministry Audit, you do not need to fill out questions 112, 113, and 114.

112. How many people live within a ten-mile radius of the church? _____
     Sixty percent of these are unchurched prospects.

113. Who are these unchurched people?
     Singles, never married _____
     Single-parent families _____
     Singles, divorced _____
     Young families _____
     Older families _____
     Middle-aged families _____
     Senior citizens _____
     Ethnic minorities _____
     Others _____

114. Which group is not being adequately ministered to in our area? (Call the churches in your area and inquire what programs they offer.)
     _____
     _____
     _____

115. Has the population of our county increased or decreased over the last ten years? _____
     By how much? _____

116. Has our church kept pace with the population increase/decrease of our county? _____

117. Are the schools full in our area? _____

Growth Principle 16

118. How many dollars and what percent of our budget do we spend on the following forms of advertising?

Yellow Pages	$ _____	Newspaper	$ _____
Flyers	$ _____	Radio	$ _____
Television	$ _____	Direct Mail	$ _____
Other	$ _____		
TOTAL	$ _____		

PERCENT OF OUR BUDGET _____%

Does the total amount represent 5 percent of our budget? _____

119. How many new families visit each week? _____
Do we contact them within forty-eight hours? _____
If so, who makes the contact?

_____

_____

_____

120. What percent of these families join our church? _____
(Multiply line 119 by 52 and divide the number into the number of new families that join each year.)

121. What brought these families to our church?
Friends and relatives _____
Driving by _____
Newspaper _____
Yellow Pages _____
Preschool _____
Singles' groups _____
Television _____
Banner _____
Direct Mail _____
Other _____

122. How many contacts are made each week with unchurched people? _____

123. Does someone on our staff work on behalf of the unchurched twenty hours each week?

_____

124. Do we make it clear in worship that we expect visitors each Sunday? _____
Does our bulletin reflect this? _____

125. How many visitors are on our mailing list each week? _____

126. Do we put visitors on the mailing list the first time they visit? _____

127. How do we collect the names of first-time visitors?

_____

_____

_____

128. Do we designate 10 percent of our parking spaces for visitors? _____

129. Do we provide information packets for visitors? _____

130. Do we have a booth or designated area for information? _____
    If so, is it well marked? _____

131. Do we have a decision booth where people can register any spiritual decision made during worship and receive help? _____

132. Is a sizable portion of our budget designed to help our leaders connect with the outside world?
    _____

Growth Principle 17

133. List budget totals for the past ten years, including operational expense and debt service (list most recent year first):

Year	Budget Total

134. Do we have a pledge drive every year for the budget? _____
    If not, do we systematically teach tithing as a spiritual discipline? _____
    If we do not use a pledge drive, what material do we use to teach tithing?

_____

_____

_____

If you do not do a pledge drive, ignore all of the following questions about pledging.

135. What time of the year is the pledge drive? _____

136. Do we have at least three weeks of education prior to taking pledges? _____

137. Does our pledge card ask only for money? _____

138. List the number and average of pledges for each of the past five years (list the most recent year first):

Year	Number of Pledges	Average Amount	Total Pledged	Budget	Percentage of Budget

139. Do our pledges underwrite no more than 70 to 90 percent of our budget? _____

140. Has the amount and the number of pledges increased or decreased each year? _____

141. Based on our records, what kind of income can we expect next year if we do nothing different?

    Pledges/current members   _____
    Pledges/new members*   _____
    Loose plate   _____
    Regular nonpledger   _____
    Building usage fees   _____
    Foundation   _____
    Special offerings   _____
    Sunday school offerings   _____
    Interest   _____
    Memorials   _____
    Other   _____
    TOTAL   _____

142. Do we select our stewardship leaders based on their giving patterns and willingness to give of themselves? _____

143. Do we contact new members for pledges? _____

144. Do we keep detailed records of giving and pledge patterns and analyze them regularly? _____

* If you discount your total pledges to reflect your historical pledge loss, then count your anticipated pledge from new members after you have divided them by two. If you do not discount the total pledges form current members, then do not count anticipated pledges from new members.

145. Is our pledge program centered around tithing? _____

146. How are campaigns conducted?

_____
_____
_____
_____
_____

147. Describe our last three stewardship programs:

_____
_____
_____
_____
_____

148. Do we encourage designated giving and discourage a unified budget? _____

149. Do we have regular special offerings for items within the budget? _____

150. Complete the following for the last ten years (most recent year first):

Year	Average Worship Attendance	Percent of Income to Average Worship Attendance*

151. Does our total budget income (operating and building) equal or exceed one thousand dollars for every person in worship on an average Sunday? (See above list.) _____

152. Does one-third of our church's income come from no more than one-fourth of our pledges? _____

_____

*Divide worship total into income total for each year.

153. Complete the following table on indebtedness for the last ten years (most recent year first):

Year	Total Debt	Total Percent of Debt to Budget*	Budgeted Debt Service (mortgage)	Percent of Debt Service to Budget**

154. Is our debt service less than 25 percent of our total operating budget? (See above list.) _____

155. List of financial resources:

Endowments   _____
Wills   _____
Capital fund pledges _____
Cash reserves   _____
Foundation   _____
Stocks and bonds   _____
Other   _____
TOTAL   _____

156. Is there a plan to use this money? _____
     If so, what is it?

     _____
     _____
     _____
     _____
     _____

157. When was the last capital fund drive? _____

158. Does the lead pastor or someone on the paid staff know what each member gives? _____

*To compute percent of indebtedness to budget, divide budget total into indebtedness totals for each year.
**To compute percent of debt service to budget, divide budget total into budgeted debt service total for each year.

Growth Principle 18

159. Does our church have a mission statement that is clear, concise, and open-ended? _____
    If so, what is it?

    _____

    _____

    _____

    _____

    _____

160. Do we have a master plan for the use of land and facilities? _____

161. List present officially adopted objectives (goals) of the church:

    _____

    _____

    _____

    _____

Growth Principle 19

162. How many people received the Official Body Survey? _____

163. How many people completed the Official Body Survey? _____

164. Do you make any changes in your schedule in the summer? _____
    If so, what are they?

    _____

    _____

    _____

    _____

    _____

Staff Readiness Survey

(D:\Surveys\Staff\Staff-Readiness.doc on the CD-ROM)

To be completed by each staff member separately. Answers are then averaged on the Totals spreadsheet on the CD-ROM (D:\Spreadsheets\Readiness Survey-Totals Spreadsheet.xls) and used in the audit (section 4).

CHURCH: _____

DATE: _____

Decide how you *feel* about the following statements and circle the appropriate number under each statement. Rate yourself on a scale of one to ten. One means that you totally agree with the statement. Ten means that you totally disagree with the statement and have no desire to change your attitude.

1. The nursery should be extra clean, neat, staffed with paid help, and open every time there is a church function.

   1   2   3   4   5   6   7   8   9   10

2. Turf issues are harmful to the growth of a church.

   1   2   3   4   5   6   7   8   9   10

3. I am willing for the facilities to be used, even if they get dirty.

   1   2   3   4   5   6   7   8   9   10

4. Reaching out to new members is just as important as taking care of the present members.

   1   2   3   4   5   6   7   8   9   10

5. I am comfortable with radical change if it will help my church reach more people for Christ.

   1   2   3   4   5   6   7   8   9   10

6. I am seldom concerned about procedure.

   1   2   3   4   5   6   7   8   9   10

7. Paying off the debt is not a major concern to me.

   1   2   3   4   5   6   7   8   9   10

8. I support the idea of spending some of the church savings in order to hire more staff or start new programs.

   1   2   3   4   5   6   7   8   9   10

9. Several worship services are fine with me because I am more interested in meeting the needs of all the people than I am in knowing everyone at church.

   1   2   3   4   5   6   7   8   9   10

10. I am not at all offended when my lead pastor does not give me regular personal attention.

    1   2   3   4   5   6   7   8   9   10

11. I realize that more staff is needed today than in the past.

    1   2   3   4   5   6   7   8   9   10

12. I always trust and affirm my lead pastor's efforts to reach more people for Christ.

    1   2   3   4   5   6   7   8   9   10

Staff Permission Giving Survey

(D:\Surveys\Staff\Staff-Permission.doc on the CD-ROM)

To be completed by *each* staff member separately. Answers are then averaged on the Totals spreadsheet on the CD-ROM (D:\Spreadsheets\Permission Giving Survey-Totals Spreadsheet.xls) and used in the audit (section 4).

Answer the following questions on a scale of one to ten with one meaning you totally agree with the statement and ten meaning you totally disagree with the statement.

1. Our church leaders believe that people doing the actual ministry should make the majority of the decisions that affect how they do their ministry.

       1   2   3   4   5   6   7   8   9   10

2. People at the lowest level of organization in our church should be able to suggest and implement improvements to their own ministry without going through several committees and levels of approval.

       1   2   3   4   5   6   7   8   9   10

3. All persons in the congregation should be free to live out their spiritual gifts in the congregation without getting approval, even if it means starting a new ministry.

       1   2   3   4   5   6   7   8   9   10

4. The nature of ministry lends itself to a team-based approach rather than to individual effort.

       1   2   3   4   5   6   7   8   9   10

5. Our leadership is flexible enough to permit restructuring or reorganization so that the organization facilitates the new mission of the church.

       1   2   3   4   5   6   7   8   9   10

6. It is possible to organize ministry so that teams can take responsibility for entire ministries.

       1   2   3   4   5   6   7   8   9   10

7. There is enough complexity in our ministry to allow for initiative and decision making.

       1   2   3   4   5   6   7   8   9   10

8. Our leadership is comfortable with individuals or teams making autonomous, on-the-spot decisions.

       1   2   3   4   5   6   7   8   9   10

9. The laity are interested in or willing to organize into teams or small groups.

       1   2   3   4   5   6   7   8   9   10

10. Our key leadership is willing to share its power with those who are not in leadership.

        1   2   3   4   5   6   7   8   9   10

11. Our church has a history of following through on new ideas.

        1   2   3   4   5   6   7   8   9   10

12. Our key lay leadership is willing to radically change its own roles and behavior.

        1   2   3   4   5   6   7   8   9   10

13. Our church is secure enough to guarantee a period of relative stability during which permission giving can develop.

        1   2   3   4   5   6   7   8   9   10

14. We have adequate resources to support and train our people.

        1   2   3   4   5   6   7   8   9   10

15. Our staff and key lay leadership understand that becoming a permission giving church is a lengthy, time-consuming, and labor-intensive process that may take five years, and are willing to make the investment in time.

        1   2   3   4   5   6   7   8   9   10

16. Our church has a network that could provide information to any layperson anytime.
     1   2   3   4   5   6   7   8   9   10

17. Our laypeople have the skills needed to take greater responsibility for the ministries of the church.
     1   2   3   4   5   6   7   8   9   10

18. Our senior/lead pastor is willing to invest in training the team leaders.
     1   2   3   4   5   6   7   8   9   10

19. Our finance and trustee committees should exist to serve the needs of those trying to implement ministry.
     1   2   3   4   5   6   7   8   9   10

20. Our leaders are more concerned with discovering ways to reach the unchurched than with how those ministries are discovered or implemented.
     1   2   3   4   5   6   7   8   9   10

Official Body Survey

(D:\Surveys\Body\Body.doc on the CD-ROM)

This questionnaire is to be completed by each member of the official administrative body.

CHURCH: _____

DATE: _____

Please have *each* member of the official body fill out this section. Answers should be rated on a scale of one to ten. One means an unqualified *yes* and ten means an unqualified *no*. Some questions logically cannot be answered in this manner and should be answered as indicated by the question. Answers will be averaged on a blank work sheet set for totals and inserted into the ministry audit.

YES   NO
1 2 3 4 5 6 7 8 9 10

1. Our lead pastor understands the everyday world of our members. _____

2. Our church deals openly with controversy. _____

3. If our official administrative body consists of more than twenty-five people, do we have an official executive committee to do the basic work? _____

4. Our leaders can articulate the implications of their relationship with Jesus Christ without sounding like bigots. _____

5. The scriptures are embodied in the daily lives of our leaders. _____

6. Called and gifted unpaid leaders teach most of our Bible studies. _____

7. Our leaders appear to be growing more like Jesus. _____

8. Our leaders serve outside the congregation as much as they serve within the congregation. _____

9. All of our leaders are in an accountability or small group. _____

10. Our leaders function like a team. _____

11. When our leaders pray, lives are touched by the presence of the Holy Spirit.   _____

12. Our leaders offer to pray for others on a regular basis. _____

13. Our leaders have a regular prayer life. _____

14. Our leaders are always open to new ways of doing ministry. _____

15. Our leaders serve out of gratitude for what God has done in their lives. _____

16. Our unpaid leaders have the skills needed to take greater responsibility for the ministries of the church. _____

17. We measure the size of our church by the number of people in worship instead of by the actual membership. _____

18. The sermons speak to our personal needs. _____

19. Our lead pastor repeats sermons for no apparent reason. _____

20. The scriptures form the basis of the sermon. _____

21. The sermons stimulate thought. _____

22. Our worship music is pleasing to a majority of the congregation. _____

23. Are we willing to have a worship service at the same time we have Sunday school? _____

24. We are willing to provide an additional service of worship even though our space may be adequate without it. _____

25. Our church understands that churches usually grow based on the leadership strengths of their lead pastors. _____

26. Our lead pastor assumes leadership for the ministry of our church. _____

27. Our lead pastor holds up for us a vision large enough to cause us to grow individually. _____

28. Our lead pastor is a leader rather than an enabler. _____

29. Our lead pastor causes things to happen in our church that would not happen otherwise. _____

30. Our lead pastor pulls us into areas of ministry that we might not go to on our own. _____

31. Our lead pastor learns from mistakes. _____

32. Our lead pastor knows how to delegate authority and he or she does so. _____

33. Our lead pastor consults us regularly about his or her vision for our church. _____

34. Our lead pastor has shown the ability to grow and develop new skills along with the growth of our church. _____

35. Our lead pastor possesses the skills needed for a church our size. _____

36. Our lead pastor can respond and relate to a wide variety of religious expressions. _____

37. Our lead pastor is able to mediate between the various factions of the church. _____

38. The main responsibility of our paid staff is to identify, recruit, equip, lead, and deploy the laity into mission. _____

39. Our lead pastor makes use of the valuable information our paid staff has about the congregation. _____

40. Our lead pastor and paid staff function as a team. _____

41. Our paid staff requires minimal supervision. _____

42. We are willing to pay higher salaries and be content with fewer paid staff members. _____

43. In relation to other churches, our church is small, medium, large, or very large. _____

44. Our lay leadership communicates to the congregation a realistic perception of our church's size and ability. _____

45. Our congregation has a realistic perception of our church's size and ability. _____

46. Our lay leadership causes the official vision of the church to happen in ways that meet the needs of the congregation. _____

47. Our lay leadership is objective on major issues and decisions. _____

48. Our lay leadership knows the difference between opinion and judgment. _____

49. Our lay leadership can suspend judgment long enough to make intelligent decisions. _____

50. Our lay leadership can accept and appreciate people with different viewpoints. _____

51. At least half of our lay leadership is new to the institutional church. _____

52. Our lay leadership is accessible to the rest of the congregation. _____

53. Our lay leadership has the necessary time and energy. _____

54. Our lay leadership causes things to happen. _____

55. Each member of our lay leadership teams has a large following in the congregation. _____

56. The tenure of our lay leadership is limited to three years. _____

57. New lay leadership surfaces on a regular basis. _____

58. We expect the following level of commitment from our members (high, medium, or low): _____

59. Our church understands that we can use only 80 percent of our space. _____

60. I have a problem finding a parking space on Sunday morning. _____
    If so, what hour do I arrive? _____

61. All of our ministries have an outreach component to them that is an entry point into the life of the congregation. _____

62. We have adequate exterior and interior signs posted around the church. _____

63. We have an adequate number of trained hosts and hostesses. _____

64. When at church, members go out of their way to meet and welcome people they do not know. _____

65. Our members pray regularly that the church will grow spiritually and numerically. _____

66. Our church talks often about money and financial stewardship. _____

67. We avoid telling people the church needs their money and instead talk about people's need to become stewards. _____

68. Our lead pastor plays the following role in the pledge drive:

    _____

    _____

    _____

69. Our church's main strength is (list only one):

    _____

    _____

    _____

70. Our church's main weakness is (list only one):

    _____

    _____

    _____

71. Our church wants to go in the following direction:

_____

_____

_____

72. The objectives of our lead pastor and the church match. _____

73. Our church is free from power cliques. _____

74. One or two people derail things that the majority wants. _____

75. The average age of the person filling out this report is: _____

76. I have been a member of this church for: _____

Official Body Readiness Survey

(D:\Surveys\Body\Body-Readiness.doc on the CD-ROM)

To be completed separately by each official body member. Answers are then averaged on the Totals spreadsheet on the CD-ROM (D:\Spreadsheets\Readiness Survey-Totals Spreadsheet.xls) and used in the audit (section 4).

Decide how you *feel* about the following statements and circle the appropriate number under each statement. Rate yourself on a scale of one to ten. One means that you totally agree with the statement. Ten means that you totally disagree with the statement and have no desire to change your attitude.

1. The nursery should be extra clean, neat, staffed with paid help, and open every time there is a church function.
   1   2   3   4   5   6   7   8   9   10

2. Turf issues are harmful to the growth of a church.
   1   2   3   4   5   6   7   8   9   10

3. I am willing for the facilities to be used, even if they get dirty.
   1   2   3   4   5   6   7   8   9   10

4. Reaching out to new members is just as important as taking care of the present members.
   1   2   3   4   5   6   7   8   9   10

5. I am comfortable with radical change if it will help my church reach more people for Christ.
   1   2   3   4   5   6   7   8   9   10

6. I am seldom concerned about procedure.
   1   2   3   4   5   6   7   8   9   10

7. Paying off the debt is not a major concern to me.
   1   2   3   4   5   6   7   8   9   10

8. I support the idea of spending some of the church's savings in order to hire more staff or start new programs.

    1   2   3   4   5   6   7   8   9   10

9. Several worship services are fine with me because I am more interested in meeting the needs of all the people than I am in knowing everyone at church.

    1   2   3   4   5   6   7   8   9   10

10. I am not at all offended when my lead pastor does not give me regular personal attention.

    1   2   3   4   5   6   7   8   9   10

11. I realize that more staff is needed today than in the past.

    1   2   3   4   5   6   7   8   9   10

12. I always trust and affirm my lead pastor's efforts to reach more people for Christ.

    1   2   3   4   5   6   7   8   9   10

Official Body Permission Giving Survey

(D:\Surveys\Body\Body-Permission.doc on the CD-ROM)

To be completed separately by *each* official body member. Answers are then averaged on Totals spreadsheet on the CD-ROM (D:\Spreadsheets\Permission Giving Survey-Totals Spreadsheet.xls) and used in the audit (section 4).

Answer the following questions on a scale of one to ten, with one meaning that you totally agree with the statement, and ten meaning that you totally disagree with the statement.

1. Our church leaders believe that people doing the actual ministry should make the majority of the decisions that affect how they do their ministry.

    1   2   3   4   5   6   7   8   9   10

2. People at the lowest level of organization in our church should be able to suggest and implement improvements to their own ministry without going through several committees and levels of approval.

    1   2   3   4   5   6   7   8   9   10

3. Each person in the congregation should be free to live out his or her spiritual gifts in the congregation without getting approval, even if it means starting a new ministry.

    1   2   3   4   5   6   7   8   9   10

4. The nature of ministry lends itself to a team-based approach rather than to individual effort.

    1   2   3   4   5   6   7   8   9   10

5. Our leadership is flexible enough to permit restructuring or reorganization in order to facilitate the new mission of the church.

    1   2   3   4   5   6   7   8   9   10

6. It is possible to organize ministry so that teams can take responsibility for entire ministries.
     1   2   3   4   5   6   7   8   9   10

7. There is enough complexity in our ministry to allow for initiative and decision making.
     1   2   3   4   5   6   7   8   9   10

8. Our leadership is comfortable with individuals or teams making autonomous, on-the-spot decisions.
     1   2   3   4   5   6   7   8   9   10

9. The laity are interested in or willing to organize into teams or small groups.
     1   2   3   4   5   6   7   8   9   10

10. Our key leadership is willing to share its power with those who are not in leadership.
     1   2   3   4   5   6   7   8   9   10

11. Our church has a history of following through on new ideas.
     1   2   3   4   5   6   7   8   9   10

12. Our key lay leadership is willing to radically change its own roles and behavior.
     1   2   3   4   5   6   7   8   9   10

13. Our church is secure enough to guarantee a period of relative stability during which permission giving can develop.
     1   2   3   4   5   6   7   8   9   10

14. We have adequate resources to support and train our people.
     1   2   3   4   5   6   7   8   9   10

15. Our staff and key lay leadership understand that becoming a permission-giving church is a lengthy, time-consuming, and labor-intensive process that may take five years, and are willing to make the investment in time.
     1   2   3   4   5   6   7   8   9   10

16. Our church has a network that could provide information to any layperson anytime.
     1   2   3   4   5   6   7   8   9   10

17. Our laypeople have the skills needed to take greater responsibility for the ministries of the church.
     1   2   3   4   5   6   7   8   9   10

18. Our senior/lead pastor is willing to invest in training the team leaders.
     1   2   3   4   5   6   7   8   9   10

19. Our finance and trustee committees should exist to serve the needs of those trying to implement ministry.
     1   2   3   4   5   6   7   8   9   10

20. Our leaders are more concerned with discovering ways to reach the unchurched than with how those ministries are discovered or implemented.
     1   2   3   4   5   6   7   8   9   10

SECTION THREE

SURVEY TOTALS

This section contains templates for totaling the scores from each of the surveys listed below.

Worship Survey Totals
Staff Survey
Readiness Survey Totals
   Staff Readiness Survey Totals
   Official Body Readiness Survey Totals
Permission Giving Survey Totals
   Staff Permission Giving Survey Totals
   Official Body Permission Giving Survey Totals
Official Body Survey

You are strongly encouraged to use the files on the CD-ROM to help you in this task. Please refer to appendix 2 for complete information on how to use the files on the CD-ROM. You will be working with the following files:

- The Body Survey Totals Spreadsheet (D:\Spreadsheets\Body Survey-Totals Spreadsheet.xls)
- The Readiness Totals Spreadsheet (D:\Spreadsheets\Readiness Survey-Totals Spreadsheet.xls)
- The Permission Giving Totals Spreadsheet (D:\Spreadsheets\Permission Giving Survey-Totals Spreadsheet.xls)
- The Worship Survey Totals Spreadsheet (D:\Spreadsheets\Worship Survey-Totals Spreadsheet.xls)

Note that there is no spreadsheet to compile the staff survey data as it is mostly informational, both current and historical.

Worship Survey Totals

After conducting the survey in worship for four consecutive Sundays, add the responses from all four weeks together, divide by four, and record the results below. A spreadsheet to help tabulate and assemble this information may be found on the bonus software CD-ROM under the filename "D:\Spreadsheets\Worship Survey-Totals Spreadsheet.xls." This spreadsheet will do all of the tedious work for you. See appendix 2 for complete information on how to use the files on the CD-ROM.

1. I was born between
    1900 and 1924_____
    1925 and 1945_____
    1946 and 1964_____
    1965 and 1984_____
    After 1984_____

2. My gender is:
   Male _____
   Female _____

3. My marital status is:
   Married _____
   Single _____

4. The number of people in my car this morning was _____.

5. The number of miles I drive or commute to church is:
   Less than one ____
   One to three ____
   Four to six ____
   Seven to ten ____
   Eleven to fifteen ____
   More than fifteen ____

6. In relation to the church, my home is in what direction?
    N___   NE___   E___   SE___   S___   SW___   W___   NW___

7. The number of miles I drive or commute to work is: _____.

8. The number of minutes I drive or commute to work is: _____.

9. What music do I listen to the most?
   Country ___
   Jazz ___
   Classical ___
   Christian ___
   Hard Rock ___
   Soft Rock ___
   Easy Listening ___
   1950–60s Music ___
   News/Talk ___
   National Public Radio ___
   Rap ___

10. I am a:
    New Visitor ___
    Continuing Visitor ___
    Member ___
    I usually attend the _____ worship service.

11. Our yearly household income is:
    Less than $7,500 ___
    $7,500 to $14,999 ___
    $15,000 to $24,999 ___
    $25,000 to $34,999___
    $35,000 to $49,999 ___
    $50,000 to $74,999 ___
    $75,000 to $99,999 ___
    $100,000 to $124,999 ___
    $125,000 or more ___

12. Are you currently in a small group at the church (fifteen people or fewer)?
    Yes _____
    No _____

13. Are you currently serving in some capacity?
    Yes _____
    No _____

14. Do you have access to electronic mail?
    Yes _____
    No _____

Staff Survey Totals

There is no need for a Staff Survey Totals template since you can just place the data directly from the Staff Survey into the Complete Ministry Audit in section 4.

Readiness Survey Totals

The Readiness Surveys measure the "heart factor" of your church. A response of one indicates total agreement with the statement and a response of ten indicates total disagreement. The lower the score, the more heart the church has for ministry to people, and the better its attitude regarding what needs to be done in order to reach the unchurched. History has shown that churches with declining attendance and vitality averaging less than three on all the questions can reverse their pattern of decline without much difficulty. Declining churches scoring an average between three and four on all questions can reverse their pattern of decline, but it will be more difficult. Those scoring an average over four on all questions have a very difficult time reaching out to the unchurched without a major change in heart and attitude.

The higher the average score on all questions, the more difficult it will be for the church to make a transition, and the slower you should go. If the score is over four, the congregation needs to spend most of the next year simply focusing on who it is and why it exists. The score on each question also predicts the difficulty the church will have initiating change in a particular area. The higher the score on each question, the more difficult it is to make changes in that area without a change of heart.

The following scores are the averages of the responses from more than 250 churches. Every church scores higher on questions 6, 7, and 8 than on the other questions.

Question	Staff	Official Body
1. Nursery	2.02	2.86
2. Turf	2.44	2.95
3. Facilities	1.84	2.48
4. Reach	1.83	1.94
5. Change	2.50	3.34
6. Procedure	4.81	5.08
7. Debt	4.27	5.46
8. Spending	3.21	4.93
9. Worship	2.00	2.42
10. Attention	2.17	2.40
11. Staff	1.62	2.35
12. Trust	1.54	1.96

Examining the following sample readiness charts will give you an idea of how to use the survey responses to get a quick overview of the church's readiness to reach out to the unchurched or pre-Christian community.

Look at the readiness chart for the average church on page 51. It shows the average staff and official body scores among more than 250 churches. Notice the following: (1) The scores of the staff are usually lower (more positive toward growth) than those of the official body. When a staff scores higher (more negative toward growth) than the official body, I know some of the staff are resistant to growth. When this occurs, it is good to examine the individual scores to see if there is one staff person skewing the scores with all nines or tens for answers; (2) The scores on questions 6, 7, and 8 for both the staff and the official body are normally higher than all the rest, forming a mountain peak on the graph. I expect these scores to be high and a problem in most churches. When they are low, I am surprised and know this is an unusual church. If the scores are significantly higher than average, I know these three areas are going to be very touchy areas for this church; and (3) There is usually a close correlation between the answers of the staff and official body. When this is not the case, I know that this is probably a good area to explore with the church leaders to see what I can learn.

The readiness chart for X Church in Any City shows the following: (1) The response to the nursery question tells me that this church does not understand the importance of a nursery. The church leaders probably no longer have any young children at home. The nursery is probably in need of a lot of work; (2) The response to the turf question tells me that it will be hard to move the nursery to a better location. More than likely, there are some locked spaces in the kitchen that only a few can use, or a parlor that children cannot enter, or some adult classes that cannot be moved; (3) The response to the attention question shows that some church leaders see their pastor as their personal chaplain. There are probably a lot of controllers in this church. When the answers to this question are above the 3.0 line, I know that there are serious problems within the staff; and (4) The response to the debt question suggests that this church will strongly resist incurring debt. I have found that there is no correlation between the amount of money a church owes and how the church answers this question. Churches with no debt will answer it just as high as churches with very high debt.

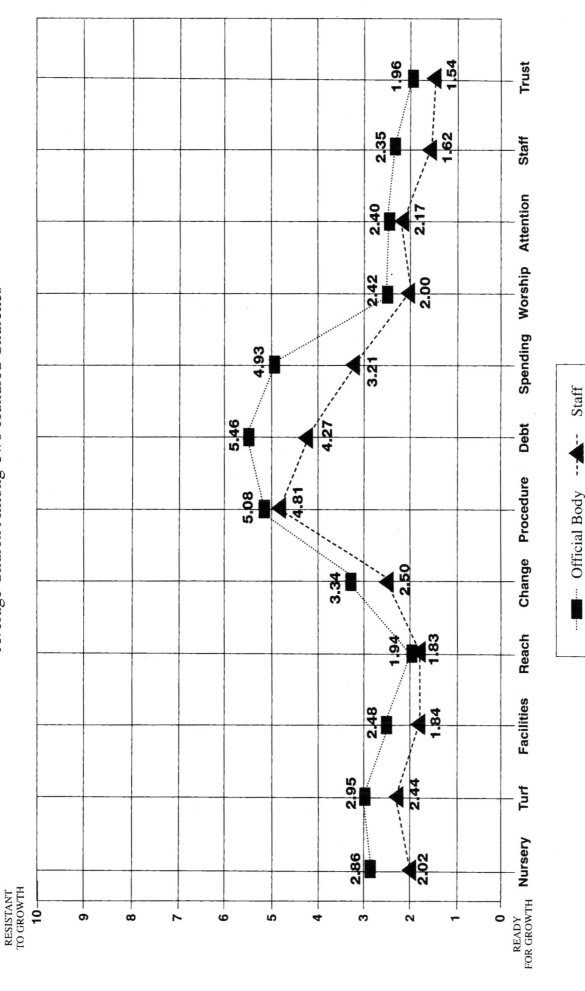

READINESS CHART
Average Church Among Two Hundred Churches

READINESS CHART
X Church, Any City

Chart categories (left to right): Nursery, Turf, Facilities, Reach, Change, Procedure, Debt, Spending, Worship, Attention, Staff, Trust

Vertical axis: 10 (top) to 0 (bottom)
- Top label: RESISTANT TO GROWTH
- Bottom label: READY FOR GROWTH

Legend:
- ···■··· Official Body
- – –▲– – Staff

Official Body values: Nursery 5.7, Turf 4.5, Facilities 1.3, Reach 1.3, Change 3.9, Procedure 5.0, Debt 7.5, Spending 5.5, Worship 1.9, Attention 3.6, Staff 2.1, Trust 2.3

Staff values: Nursery 1.0, Turf 1.5, Facilities 1.0, Reach 1.0, Change 1.5, Procedure 2.5, Debt 2.5, Spending 1.0, Worship 1.0, Attention 1.0, Staff 1.0, Trust 1.0

Staff Readiness Survey Totals

Average the paid staff's responses to the Staff Readiness Survey and record them below. This total sheet can be found on the bonus CD-ROM under the filename "D:\Spreadsheets\Readiness Survey-Totals Spreadsheet.xls." The totals can be averaged in the spreadsheet. Please note that the spreadsheet totals information for both staff and the official body.

1. The nursery should be extra clean, neat, staffed with paid help, and open every time there is a church function.
   Average of responses: _____

2. Turf issues are harmful to the growth of a church.
   Average of responses: _____

3. I am willing for the facilities to be used, even if they get dirty.
   Average of responses: _____

4. Reaching out to new members is just as important as taking care of the present members.
   Average of responses: _____

5. I am comfortable with radical change if it will help my church reach more people for Christ.
   Average of responses: _____

6. I am seldom concerned about procedure.
   Average of responses: _____

7. Paying off the debt is not a major concern to me.
   Average of responses: _____

8. I support the idea of spending some of the church savings in order to hire more staff or start new programs.
   Average of responses: _____

9. Several worship services are fine with me because I am more interested in meeting the needs of all the people than I am in knowing everyone at church.
   Average of responses: _____

10. I am not at all offended when my lead pastor does not give me regular personal attention.
    Average of responses: _____

11. I realize that more staff is needed today than in the past.
    Average of responses: _____

12. I always trust and affirm my lead pastor's efforts to reach more people for Christ.
    Average of responses: _____

Official Body Readiness Survey Totals

Average the official body's responses to the Official Body Readiness Survey and record them below. This total sheet can be found on the bonus CD-ROM under the filename "D:\Spreadsheets\Readiness

Survey-Totals Spreadsheet.xls." Please note that the spreadsheet totals information for both staff and the official body.

1. The nursery should be extra clean, neat, staffed with paid help, and open every time there is a church function.
   Average of responses: _____

2. Turf issues are harmful to the growth of a church.
   Average of responses: _____

3. I am willing for the facilities to be used, even if they get dirty.
   Average of responses: _____

4. Reaching out to new members is just as important as taking care of the present members.
   Average of responses: _____

5. I am comfortable with radical change if it will help my church reach more people for Christ.
   Average of responses: _____

6. I am seldom concerned about procedure.
   Average of responses: _____

7. Paying off the debt is not a major concern to me.
   Average of responses: _____

8. I support the idea of spending some of our church's savings in order to hire more staff or start new programs.
   Average of responses: _____

9. Several worship services are fine with me because I am more interested in meeting the needs of all the people than I am in knowing everyone at church.
   Average of responses: _____

10. I am not at all offended when my lead pastor does not give me regular personal attention.
    Average of responses: _____

11. I realize that more staff is needed today than in the past.
    Average of responses: _____

12. I always trust and affirm my lead pastor's efforts to reach more people for Christ.
    Average of responses: _____

Permission Giving Survey Totals

The lower the score on each of these questions, the more able the church is to transform into a permission-giving church. If the total for all scores is less than sixty, you are already a permission-giving church or are ready to become a permission-giving church. If the total for all scores is between sixty-one and seventy-nine, you have some weaknesses in your permission-giving system. Work on the weaknesses and begin the shift gradually. If the total for all scores is more than eighty, it is too early to begin trying to transform the church. Begin exploring your mission, vision, and value statements.

A permission-giving church empowers people to make on-the-spot decisions and develop new ministries without asking permission from the official body. Each person is held accountable for her or his actions, based on the mission, vision, and value statements of the church. This church is more concerned with sharing the gospel by responding to the heartfelt needs of people in the name of Jesus Christ than with following certain procedures or controlling what people can or cannot do.

A permission-giving church is based on trust, collaboration, and networks. It is organized to ensure that old and new ministries take place. The organization focuses on personal and corporate growth instead of institutional growth. This church stresses the spiritual gifts of each person instead of finding people to fill the offices of the church. Chaos is seen as good. New ministries are more important than perpetuating the status quo. Too many churches are organized to prevent anything bad from happening or someone going off on a tangent; as a result of this kind of overcautious organization, they ensure that nothing happens.

Permission-giving churches believe that the role of God's people is to minister to people, in the world, every day of the week, by living out their spiritual gifts instead of running the church by sitting on committees and making decisions about what can or cannot be done. This church seeks unity in the essentials, freedom in the nonessentials, and trust and love in all things. The key elements are empowerment, responsibility, trust, a common mission, freedom, autonomy, decentralization, networks, synergy, and the collaboration of individuals and teams.

In a permission-giving church, the role of laity is to live out their spiritual gifts. People are not asked routinely to serve on committees. Networks encourage autonomous, on-the-spot decision making by individuals and self-organizing, self-governing, self-destructing teams. They encourage ministry to be delivered anytime, anyplace, by anyone, no matter what. They do not give a new ministry to an existing committee to implement. They avoid taking a vote on new ministries whenever possible. They bless diversity more than uniformity and are passionate about providing choices. Representative democracy is unimportant. They have leaders who are secure enough to equip others for ministry, and then get out of their way and let them develop their ministry, even if it is not something in which they might participate. Permission-giving churches do need boundaries other than the mission, vision, and value statements. Permission-giving churches develop a flat organizational structure that encourages and facilitates ministry instead of coordinating or managing it. The organization's first goal is to help people grow in their faith, not to "run the church." For more information on how the permission-giving church works, see Bill Easum's *Sacred Cows Make Gourmet Burgers*.

Staff Permission Giving Survey Totals

Average the paid staff's responses to the Staff Permission Giving Survey and record them below. This total sheet can be found on the bonus CD-ROM under the filename "D:\Spreadsheets\Permission Giving Survey-Totals Spreadsheet.xls." Please note that the spreadsheet totals information for both staff and the official body.

1. Our church leaders believe that people doing the actual ministry should make the majority of the decisions that affect how they do their ministry.
   Average of responses: _____

2. People at the lowest level of organization in our church should be able to suggest and implement improvements to their own ministry without going through several committees and levels of approval.
   Average of responses: _____

3. All persons in the congregation should be free to live out their spiritual gifts in the congregation without getting approval, even if it means starting a new ministry.
Average of responses: _____

4. The nature of ministry lends itself to a team-based approach rather than to individual effort.
Average of responses: _____

5. Our leadership is flexible enough to permit restructuring or reorganization so that the organization facilitates the new mission of the church.
Average of responses: _____

6. It is possible to organize ministry so that teams can take responsibility for entire ministries.
Average of responses: _____

7. There is enough complexity in our ministry to allow for initiative and decision making.
Average of responses: _____

8. Our leadership is comfortable with individuals or teams making autonomous, on-the-spot decisions.
Average of responses: _____

9. The laity are interested in or willing to organize into teams or small groups.
Average of responses: _____

10. Our key leadership is willing to share its power with those who are not in leadership.
Average of responses: _____

11. Our church has a history of following through on new ideas.
Average of responses: _____

12. Our key lay leadership is willing to radically change its own roles and behavior.
Average of responses: _____

13. Our church is secure enough to guarantee a period of relative stability during which permission giving can develop.
Average of responses: _____

14. We have adequate resources to support and train our people.
Average of responses: _____

15. Our staff and key lay leadership understand that becoming a permission-giving church is a lengthy, time-consuming, and labor-intensive process that may take five years and are willing to make the investment in time.
Average of responses: _____

16. Our church has a network that could provide information to any layperson anytime.
Average of responses: _____

17. Our laypeople have the skills needed to take greater responsibility for the ministries of the church.
Average of responses: _____

18. Our senior/lead pastor is willing to invest in training the team leaders.
Average of responses: _____

19. Our finance and trustee committees should exist to serve the needs of those trying to implement ministry.
Average of responses: _____

20. Our leaders are more concerned with discovering ways to reach the unchurched than with how those ministries are discovered or implemented.
Average of responses: _____

Official Body Permission Giving Survey Totals

Average the official body's responses to the Official Body Permission Giving Survey and record them below. This total sheet can be found on the bonus CD-ROM under the filename "D:\Spreadsheets\Permission Giving Survey-Totals Spreadsheet.xls." Please note that the spreadsheet totals information for both staff and the official body.

1. Our church leaders believe that people doing the actual ministry should make the majority of the decisions that affect how they do their ministry.
Average of responses: _____

2. People at the lowest level of organization in our church should be able to suggest and implement improvements to their own ministry without going through several committees and levels of approval.
Average of responses: _____

3. All persons in the congregation should be free to live out their spiritual gifts in the congregation without getting approval, even if it means starting a new ministry.
Average of responses: _____

4. The nature of ministry lends itself to a team-based approach rather than to individual effort.
Average of responses: _____

5. Our leadership is flexible enough to permit restructuring or reorganization so that the organization facilitates the new mission of the church.
Average of responses: _____

6. It is possible to organize ministry so that teams can take responsibility for entire ministries.
Average of responses: _____

7. There is enough complexity in our ministry to allow for initiative and decision making.
Average of responses: _____

8. Our leadership is comfortable with individuals or teams making autonomous, on-the-spot decisions.
Average of responses: _____

9. The laity are interested in or willing to organize into teams or small groups.
Average of responses: _____

10. Our key leadership is willing to share its power with those who are not in leadership.
Average of responses: _____

11. Our church has a history of following through on new ideas.
Average of responses: _____

12. Our key lay leadership is willing to radically change its own roles and behavior.
Average of responses: _____

13. Our church is secure enough to guarantee a period of relative stability during which permission giving can develop.
Average of responses: _____

14. We have adequate resources to support and train our people.
Average of responses: _____

15. Our staff and key lay leadership understand that becoming a permission-giving church is a lengthy, time-consuming, and labor-intensive process that may take five years, and are willing to make the investment in time.
Average of responses: _____

16. Our church has a network that could provide information to any layperson anytime.
Average of responses: _____

17. Our laypeople have the skills needed to take greater responsibility for the ministries of the church.
Average of responses: _____

18. Our senior/lead pastor is willing to invest in training the team leaders.
Average of responses: _____

19. Our finance and trustee committees should exist to serve the needs of those trying to implement ministry.
Average of responses: _____

20. Our leaders are more concerned with discovering ways to reach the unchurched than with how those ministries are discovered or implemented.
Average of responses: _____

Official Body Survey Totals

(The Official Body Survey Totals section is to be completed by whoever is in charge of compiling the data.)

This total sheet can be found on the bonus CD-ROM under the filename "D:\Spreadsheets\Body Survey-Totals Spreadsheet.xls."

CHURCH: _____

DATE: _____

Please record the average of each of the collated data collected from the respondents from the official body. The statements have been divided up according to Growth Principles to aid you in finding the correct place to insert the averages.

Growth Principle 1

1. Our lead pastor understands the everyday world of our members.

2. Our church deals openly with controversy.

3. If our official administrative body consists of more than twenty-five people, do we have an official executive committee to do the basic work?

(There are no questions for Growth Principles 2 through 5.)

Growth Principle 6

4. Our leaders can articulate the implications of their relationship with Jesus Christ without sounding like bigots.

5. The scriptures are embodied in the daily lives of our leaders.

6. Called and gifted unpaid leaders teach most of our Bible studies.

7. Our leaders appear to be growing more like Jesus.

8. Our leaders serve outside the congregation as much as they serve within the congregation.

9. All of our leaders are in an accountability or small group.

10. Our leaders function like a team.

11. When our leaders pray, lives are touched by the presence of the Holy Spirit.

12. Our leaders offer to pray for others on a regular basis.

13. Our leaders have a regular prayer life.

14. Our leaders are always open to new ways of doing ministry.

15. Our leaders serve out of gratitude for what God has done in their lives.

16. Our unpaid leaders have the skills needed to take greater responsibility for the ministries of the church.

Growth Principle 7

17. We measure the size of our church by the number of people in worship instead of by the actual membership.

18. The sermons speak to our personal needs.

19. Our lead pastor repeats sermons for no apparent reason.

20. The scriptures form the basis of the sermon.

21. The sermons stimulate thought.

22. Our worship music is pleasing to a majority of the congregation.

Growth Principle 8

23. We are willing to have a worship service at the same time we have Sunday school.

24. We are willing to provide an additional service of worship even though our space may be adequate without it.

Growth Principle 9

25. Our church understands that churches usually grow based on the leadership strengths of the lead pastors.

26. Our lead pastor assumes leadership for the ministry of our church.

27. Our lead pastor holds up for us a vision large enough to cause us to grow individually.

28. Our lead pastor is a leader rather than an enabler.

29. Our lead pastor causes things to happen in our church that would not happen otherwise.

30. Our lead pastor pulls us into areas of ministry that we might not go to on our own.

31. Our lead pastor learns from mistakes.

32. Our lead pastor knows how to delegate authority and he or she does so.

33. Our lead pastor consults us regularly about his or her vision for our church.

34. Our lead pastor has shown the ability to grow and develop new skills along with the growth of our church.

35. Our lead pastor possesses the skills needed for a church our size.

36. Our lead pastor can respond and relate to a wide variety of religious expressions.

37. Our lead pastor is able to mediate between the various factions of the church.

Growth Principle 10

38. The main responsibility of our paid staff is to identify, recruit, equip, lead, and deploy the laity into mission.

39. Our lead pastor makes use of the valuable information our paid staff has about the congregation.

40. Our lead pastor and paid staff function as a team.

41. Our paid staff requires minimal supervision.

42. We are willing to pay higher salaries and be content with fewer paid staff.

Growth Principle 11

43. In relation to other churches, our church is small, medium, large, or very large.

44. Our lay leadership communicates to the congregation a realistic perception of our church's size and ability.

45. Our congregation has a realistic perception of our church's size and ability.

46. Our lay leadership causes the official vision of the church to happen in ways that meet the needs of the congregation.

47. Our lay leadership is objective on major issues and decisions.

48. Our lay leadership knows the difference between opinion and judgment.

49. Our lay leadership can suspend judgment long enough to make intelligent decisions.

50. Our lay leadership can accept and appreciate people with different viewpoints.

51. At least half of our lay leadership is new to the institutional church.

52. Our lay leadership is accessible to the rest of the congregation.

53. Our lay leadership has the necessary time and energy.

54. Our lay leadership causes things to happen.

55. Each member of our lay leadership teams has a large following in the congregation.

56. The tenure of our lay leadership is limited to three years.

57. New lay leadership surfaces on a regular basis.

Growth Principle 12

58. We expect the following level of commitment from our members:
high, medium, or low

59. Our church understands that we can use only 80 percent of our space.

Growth Principle 13

60. I have a problem finding a parking space on Sunday morning.
    If so, what hour do you arrive?

(No questions for Growth Principles 14 or 15.)

Growth Principle 16

61. All of our ministries have an outreach component to them that is an entry point into the life of the congregation.

62. We have adequate exterior and interior signs posted around the church.

63. We have an adequate number of trained hosts and hostesses.

64. When at church, members go out of their way to meet and welcome people they do not know.

65. Our members pray regularly that the church will grow spiritually and numerically.

Growth Principle 17

66. Our church talks often about money and financial stewardship.

67. We avoid telling people the church needs their money and instead talk about people's need to become stewards.

68. Our lead pastor plays the following role in the pledge drive:

Growth Principle 18

69. Our church's main strength is (list only one):

70. Our church's main weakness is (list only one):

71. Our church wants to go in the following direction:

Growth Principle 19

72. The objectives of our lead pastor and church match.

73. Our church is free from power cliques.

74. One or two people derail things that the majority wants.

75. My age is (average for Ministry Audit):

76. I have been a member of this church for:

SECTION FOUR

THE COMPLETE MINISTRY AUDIT

Options for Using the Ministry Audit

Once you have completed *The Complete Ministry Audit,* you have several options as to how you proceed.

- Request an on-site consultation with Bill Easum
- Request an audit by mail
- Do the audit yourself

Of course the best way to complete the study is to contact our office and set up an on-site visit. The size of the church determines the number of days needed for the on-site visit. If you wish to pursue this option, call 361-749-5364 or e-mail us at easum@easumbandy.com.

If you decide to do the audit by mail, then e-mail us at easum@easumbandy.com and we will give you the details.

If you decide to do the audit yourself, give careful attention to the action items listed in each Growth Principle in the study guide. You might also give careful attention to two books, *The Church Growth Handbook* and *Unfreezing Moves,* by Bill Easum.

Have fun!

Bill Easum

The Ministry Audit

This section contains a copy of the blank Ministry Audit that the steering team will fill out and distribute with their report. Make a photocopy of it now so that you can use the blank audit again at another time. We recommend, however, that you use the Growth Principle Templates on the CD-ROM to enter and organize the data. Use the files "D:\Growth Principles\Growth Principle 1.doc" through "D:\Growth Principles\Growth Principle 19.doc." All of the information to enter into the audit and the Growth Principle Templates comes from the Surveys and Survey Totals in sections 2 and 3.

Complete instructions for using the files on the CD-ROM are given in appendix 2.

When this document is completed, it will be distributed to everyone who is using the study guide. It should also be distributed with the final report when the steering team makes its final recommendations.

Two kinds of questions are comprised in the Ministry Audit. First, the numbers marked by an asterisk (*) are to be answered on a scale of one to ten, with one indicating total agreement or an absolute yes. These questions are to be answered by the administrative body of the church. They are subjective questions that deal with perception and, therefore, have no right or wrong answers. We have supplied the average scores for all of the questions marked by an asterisk. These averages come from the scores of more than 250 churches throughout the United States. (For approximate averages for Canadian churches, add .30 to all of the answers.) Any score that is more than .50 above the average is outside of the norm for that answer, either positively or negatively. Second, the questions that are not marked with an asterisk deal with fact more than perception and are compiled from the various records in the church or the survey taken in worship.

Growth Principle 1: Growth Is Not Concerned with Numbers but with Growing Disciples

1. What is the age, gender, and marital status of adult worshippers? (Compiled from the Worship Survey, question 1).
M/M=male/married, M/S=male/single, F/M=female/married, F/S=female/single.

Born between 1900 and 1924		Born between 1925 and 1945		Born between 1946 and 1964		Born between 1965 and 1984		Born after 1984			
No.:	___	No.:	___	No.:	___	No.:	___	No.:	___	No.:	___
%:	___	%:	___	%:	___	%:	___	%:	___		
M/M	___	M/M	___	M/M	___	M/M	___	M/M	___	Male:	___
M/S	___	M/S	___	M/S	___	M/S	___	M/S	___	Female:	___
F/M	___	F/M	___	F/M	___	F/M	___	F/M	___	Married:	___
F/S	___	F/S	___	F/S	___	F/S	___	F/S	___	Single:	___

What are the population statistics (broken down by age) for our area? (Contact the Chamber of Commerce for this information if your church did not order Percept.)

Percentage Born Between:
1900 and 1924____%   1925 and 1945_____%   1946 and 1964____%   1965 and 1984___%
After 1984___%

Based on this comparison, on what age group do we need to concentrate? _____

*2. Our lead pastor understands the everyday world of our members. (2.73) _____

3. What are our people programs, including specialized ministries?

_____

_____

_____

_____

_____

*Children and youth are not included in the survey because they generally do not make decisions in congregations.

4. Has there been any major controversy or division in the last five years?

_____

_____

_____

_____

_____

*5. Our church deals openly with controversy. (4.81) _____

6. What is our decision-making process?

_____

_____

_____

_____

*7. If our official administrative body consists of more than twenty-five people, do we have an official executive committee to do the basic work? (5.32) _____

8. Who gives or withholds permission for new ideas or ministries in our church?

_____

_____

_____

_____

9. What is our church known for on the community grapevine?

_____

_____

_____

_____

10. Describe our local church organizational structure.

_____

_____

_____

_____

_____

Growth Principle 2: Growth Occurs When People Are Given a Wide Variety of Choices

1. Does our church offer a balanced ministry? _____

List the various programs under the following headings:

Love (Nurture)	Justice (Social Action)	Mercy (Evangelism)
_____	_____	_____
_____	_____	_____
_____	_____	_____
_____	_____	_____
_____	_____	_____

2. Does our church have a preschool? _____
   How many attend? _____

3. Does our church have a grade school? _____
   How many attend? _____

4. Does our church have a parent's day out program? _____
   How many attend? _____

5. Does our church have a day care? _____
   How many attend? _____

6. Does our church have adult day care? _____
   How many attend? _____

7. Do we start a new Sunday school class every three to six months? _____

8. Number of adult Sunday school classes: _____
   How many attend? _____

9. Number of singles' Sunday school classes: _____
   How many attend? _____

10. Number of youth Sunday school classes: _____
    How many attend? _____

11. Number of children's Sunday school classes: _____
    How many attend? _____

12. When was the newest adult Sunday school class started? _____

13. Does our church have Sunday evening programs? _____
    If so, please list them and include approximate attendance:

_____

_____

_____

14. Does our church have midweek programs? _____
    If so, please list them and include approximate attendance:_____

_____

_____

_____

15. Does our church have Bible studies? _____
    If so, please list them and include approximate attendance:_____

_____

_____

_____

16. Does our church have athletic programs? _____
    If so, please list them: _____

_____

_____

_____

_____

17. Does our church have a mentoring program? _____

18. List any other programs: _____

_____

_____

_____

_____

Growth Principle 3: Growth Occurs When People Are Matched with Their Gifts and Skills

1. What is our nominating process?

_____

_____

_____

_____

2. Do we encourage and use spiritual gifts inventories? _____
   If so, describe the material and the process:

_____

_____

_____

_____

Growth Principle 4: Growth Does Not Dictate That More People Will Become Inactive

1. List the membership figures for the last ten years, with the most recent year first.

Year	Membership

2. List our membership losses for the last ten years, with the most recent year first.

Year	Death	Withdrawal	Transfer to Same Denomination	Transfer to Other Denomination	Total

3. Do we concentrate on assimilating new members within the first three months? _____

4. Is a staff person or volunteer responsible for the assimilation of new members? _____

5. Does our church have enough small groups for the size of our church? _____
   You need one small group for every ten people in worship.
   To determine this number:
   a. Divide worship attendance by ten; _____
   b. Count the number of small groups with fifteen or fewer in attendance (include Sunday school classes); _____
   c. Subtract line a from line b to determine the number over or under what is needed. _____

6. List the number of each of the following small groups (do not count Sunday school classes):
   a. Recovery _____
   b. Support _____
   c. Learning _____
   d. Mission or discipling _____
   e. Institutional (required denominational) _____

7. What percent of the congregation is inactive? _____

8. Have we cleaned our rolls within the last three years? _____

9. Describe our assimilation program:

   _____

   _____

   _____

   _____

Growth Principle 5: Growth Provides a Wider Outreach to People in Need

1. List the amount of money given to all causes outside our congregation for the past ten years. Include all denominational requirements. List the most recent year first.

Year	Amount Given

Growth Principle 6: Spiritual Leadership Is Required

(The term *leaders* refers to every leader in the church, paid or unpaid.)

1. Our leaders can articulate the implications of their relationship with Jesus Christ without sounding like bigots. _____

2. The scriptures are embodied in the daily lives of our leaders. _____

3. Called and gifted unpaid leaders teach most of our Bible studies. _____

4. Our leaders appear to be growing more like Jesus. _____

5. Our leaders serve outside the congregation as much as they serve within the congregation. _____

6. All of our leaders are in an accountability or small group. _____

7. Our leaders function like a team. _____

8. When our leaders pray, lives are touched by the presence of the Holy Spirit. _____

9. Our leaders offer to pray for others on a regular basis. _____

10. Our leaders have a regular prayer life. _____

11. Our leaders are always open to new ways of doing ministry. _____

12. Our leaders serve out of gratitude for what God has done in their lives. _____

13. Our unpaid leaders have the skills needed to take greater responsibility for the ministries of the church. _____

Growth Principle 7: Growth Will Occur When Worship Is Intentionally Emphasized

*1. We measure the size of our church by the number of people in worship instead of by the actual membership. (4.48) _____

2. How many Sundays a year is there a sermon from our lead pastor? _____

3. Do we regularly have different pastors preach or do we have more than one pastor preach each week? _____

4. How many Sundays a year does the service contain a sermon? _____

5. How many Sundays a year is there a sermon from our associate pastor? _____

*6. The sermons speak to our personal needs. (2.46) _____

*7. Our lead pastor repeats sermons for no apparent reason. (9.32) _____

*8. The scriptures form the basis of the sermon. (1.76) _____

*9. The sermons stimulate thought. (2.07) _____

*10. Our worship music is pleasing to a majority of the congregation. (2.00) _____

11. List the size of our present adult and youth choir(s) and the number of hours they sing. (Note if it is a choir, praise band, or band. Do not include children's choirs.)

Choir	Service	Present Size	Ideal Size†

12. What is the percentage of worship attendance to membership? _____

13. Do we have an attendance tracking system? _____
    Do we use it? _____
    If so, how?

_____

_____

_____

_____

14. Analysis of worship growth pattern for the last ten years. List the most current year first.

Year	Average Attendance			Total	Percent Increase (+) or Decrease (-)
	Service #1	Service #2	Service #3		

Worship has increased/decreased _____% in the past ten years.
(Determine percentage of growth each year. For example, take the amount of difference between years one and two and divide it by year one.)

†To determine the ideal size for each choir for each service, divide the attendance for each service at which the choir sings by ten.

15. Do we use multimedia in our worship on a weekly basis? _____

Growth Principle 8: Growth Will Occur with the Addition of Each New Morning Service of Worship

1. How many Sunday morning worship services do we have, and what are their hours?

   _____   _____   _____

2. Average attendance at each: _____   _____   _____

3. Do we have worship at any other time of the week? _____
   If so, when? _____

4. Do we have any satellite services? _____
   If so, how do we accomplish them?

   _____

   _____

   _____

   _____

5. If offering more than one service, does the same pastor preach each service, or is there a choice of speakers? If using more than one speaker, please describe:

   _____

   _____

   _____

   _____

*6. Are we willing to have a worship service at the same time we have Sunday school? (5.36) _____

7. When was the newest service started? _____
   Which one was it? _____

*8. We are willing to provide an additional service of worship even though our space may be adequate without it. (3.10) _____

9. Does each service have a regular choir or band? _____
   If not, which ones do not? _____

10. Is there a youth choir that sings regularly? _____

11. How many Sundays a year does our major adult choir sing? _____

12. Does our major adult choir take a vacation? _____

13. How many children's choirs does our church have? _____
    How often do they sing? _____

14. How many Christmas Eve services does our church have? _____

Describe each service, and list the hours that each service is offered:

_____

_____

_____

_____

_____

_____

Growth Principle 9: Growth Is Directly Related to the Leadership Strength of the Pastor

*1. Our church understands that churches usually grow based on the leadership strengths of their lead pastors. (2.64) _____

*2. Our lead pastor assumes leadership for the ministry of our church. (1.59) _____

3. What is the average tenure of all lead pastors in the last twenty years? _____

4. Tenure of present lead pastor: _____

5. How much vacation do our pastors and staff receive? _____

*6. Our lead pastor holds up for us a vision large enough to cause us to grow individually. (2.47) _____

*7. Our lead pastor is a leader rather than an enabler. (2.55) _____

*8. Our lead pastor causes things to happen in our church that would not happen otherwise. (2.05) _____

*9. Our lead pastor pulls us into areas of ministry that we might not go to on our own. (2.51) _____

*10. Our lead pastor learns from mistakes. (2.25) _____

*11. Our lead pastor knows how to delegate authority and he or she does so. (2.46) _____

*12. Our lead pastor consults us regularly about his or her vision for our church. (2.45) _____

*13. Our lead pastor has shown the ability to grow and develop new skills along with the growth of the church. (2.30) _____

*14. Our lead pastor possesses the skills needed for a church our size. (1.80) _____

*15. Our lead pastor can respond and relate to a wide variety of religious expressions. (2.01) _____

*16. Our lead pastor is able to mediate between the various factions of the church. (2.49) _____

Growth Principle 10: Growth Is Directly Related to the Attitude of the Paid Staff

*1. The main responsibility of our paid staff is to identify, recruit, equip, lead, and deploy the laity into mission. (4.97) _____

2. Number of present staff (On a separate piece of paper, please list all the paid staff, listing name, job title, salary, length of service, and whether the person serves full-time or part-time. Add up program staff and support staff, not by the actual number of people but by how the total equates to full-time positions. Example: two persons serving half-time equal one full-time person.): _____

   Program Staff—Full-time: _____
   Program Staff—Part-time: _____
   Total full-time program staff (add up the part-time people): _____
   Support Staff—Full-time: _____
   Support Staff—Part-time: _____
   Total Support Staff (add up the part-time people): _____

3. Has the number of staff kept pace with the growth of the church? _____

4. We are staffed for *Decline, Maintenance,* or *Growth* based on the answer to question 2: _____

5. Is the role of our associate pastor that of apprentice, professional, or retired? _____

*6. Our lead pastor makes use of the valuable information our paid staff has about the congregation. (2.74) _____

7. Our lead pastor and paid staff function as a team. _____

8. Is there adequate continuing education money in the budget for each paid staff member? _____

9. Does our paid staff hold weekly staff meetings? _____
   If so, on a separate piece of paper, describe a typical staff meeting. _____

10. Does each paid staff member have an opportunity to have input into the staff agenda? _____

11. Are new ideas welcome at the staff meetings from the paid staff? _____

12. Does the paid staff have yearly retreats? _____

13. Does the paid staff gather on Sunday mornings to make sure all bases are covered? _____

*14. Our paid staff requires minimal supervision. (2.79) _____

*15. We are willing to pay higher salaries and be content with fewer paid staff. (5.14) _____

16. What percent of our budget do our salaries represent? _____

17. Is there a certain time each week set aside by the lead pastor during which individual paid staff members can make appointments to consult with the pastor? _____

18. Does the lead pastor share his or her vision for the congregation at the staff meetings? _____

19. Has our staff had formal training in time management? _____

Growth Principle 11: Growth Is Directly Related to the Unpaid Staff's Perception of the Congregation's Size and Ability Rather than Reality

1. Use the following chart to determine the actual size of our church in relation to other Protestant churches.

Average Worship Attendance	Percent of Churches
1-49	40.5%
50-74	57.5%
75-99	69.1%
100-149	81.6%
150-199	88.6%
200-349	96.3%
350-499	98.4%
500-749	99.3%
750-999	99.6%
1000+	99.7%

Based on these figures, our church is larger than _____% of all Protestant churches. (These figures may vary a few percentage points from denomination to denomination.)

2. In relation to other churches our church is: small, medium, large, or very large. _____

3. Is our leadership's perception of our church's size the same as the reality of our church's size? (compare question 2 to question 1) _____

*4. Our lay leadership communicates to the congregation a realistic perception of our church's size and ability. (4.21) _____

*5. Our congregation has a realistic perception of our church's size and ability. (4.69) _____

*6. Our lay leadership causes the official vision of the church to happen in ways that meet the needs of the congregation. (4.31) _____

*7. Our lay leadership is objective on major issues and decisions. (4.13) _____

*8. Our lay leadership knows the difference between opinion and judgment. (3.89) _____

*9. Our lay leadership can suspend judgment long enough to make intelligent decisions. (3.49) _____

*10. Our lay leadership can accept and appreciate people with different viewpoints. (3.63) _____

*11. At least half of our lay leadership is new to the institutional church. (6.34) _____

*12. Our lay leadership is accessible to the rest of the congregation. (2.87) _____

*13. Our lay leadership has the necessary time and energy. (3.59) _____

*14. Our lay leadership causes things to happen. (3.57) _____

*15. Each member of our lay leadership teams has a large following in the congregation. (4.53) _____

*16. The tenure of our lay leadership is limited to three years. (5.17) _____

*17. New lay leadership surfaces on a regular basis. (4.45) _____

18. What is our greatest challenge in developing lay leaders? Recruiting? Equipping? Identifying? Deploying? _____

19. How do we raise up leaders?

_____

_____

_____

_____

Growth Principle 12: When 80 Percent of Any Space Is in Use, It Is Time to Start Making Plans for More Space

1. We expect the following level of commitment from our members (high, medium, or low): _____

2. In the past, has our church missed any "windows of opportunity"? _____
    If so, what were they?

_____

_____

_____

_____

_____

*3. Our church understands that we can use only 80 percent of our space. (6.84) _____

4. Do we need more worship space? _____
(Do not estimate or rely solely on an architect's estimate. Measure the capacity of your sanctuary by actually counting how many people can sit on a pew comfortably and then compute a total by multiplying this number by the number of pews throughout the sanctuary. Another option is to measure actual pew length and divide by twenty-two inches.)

a. Sanctuary capacity: _____
b. 80 percent capacity: _____
c. Average attendance at largest service: _____
(If c is larger than b, you need more worship space.)

5. Is our worship capacity more than 50 percent larger than our Sunday school capacity? _____
(To get the answer, compare question 4a with question 8b.)

6. Do we need more choir space? _____
a. Choir space capacity: _____
b. 80 percent of capacity: _____
c. Average main attendance: _____
(If c is larger than b, the answer to question 6 is yes.)

7. Do we need more nursery space? _____
a. Nursery capacity: _____
b. 80 percent of capacity: _____
c. Average main attendance: _____
(If c is larger than b, the answer to question 7 is yes.)

How many nursery personnel are on duty for the largest worship service? _____

Is there a nursery for all events? _____

Are infants and toddlers separated? _____

Are there any written nursery policies that are given to the parents? _____

Do we have adequate security in place to avoid noncustodial kidnapping? _____

Do we offer pagers to first-time users of our nursery? _____

8. Do we need more education space? _____

Allow thirty square feet per person for students kindergarten age and younger; twenty square feet per person for those in first grade or above. From this figure, calculate the education capacity.
a. Education capacity: _____
b. 80 percent of capacity: _____
c. Average main attendance: _____
(If c is larger than b, the answer to question 8 is yes.)

9. Is each one of our Sunday school classes at less than 80 percent of the capacity for its space? _____

10. Which classes are at greater than 80 percent of capacity?

_____

_____

_____

_____

Do we need to rearrange any of these classes? _____

11. Number of classrooms available: _____
    Number of classrooms presently used: _____

12. List the total Sunday school average attendance and percent of growth for each of the last ten years (most recent year first).

Year	Average Attendance	Percent Increase (+) or Decrease (-)

Sunday school attendance has increased/decreased _____% in the last ten years.

13. Do we have more than one session of Sunday school? _____

    If so, please list times and attendance of each:

    _____

    _____

    _____

    _____

    _____

14. According to the 80 percent rule, does our church need to add space? _____

    If so, where?

    _____

    _____

    _____

    _____

    _____

Growth Principle 13: Growth Is Encouraged When Parking Is Adequate

1. Does our church own enough land? _____

   If we currently own fewer than ten acres, is there adjacent property for sale? _____
   We own: _____
   We need: _____

2. What is the average attendance of the largest worship service? _____
   If Sunday school and worship occur at the same hour, count the total number in attendance at that hour if this combined total is larger than other worship service attendance.

3. Average number of people per car: _____

4. Number of paved off-street parking spaces available (please count): _____

5. Eighty percent of this number of parking spaces is: _____

6. Number of spaces needed to accommodate attendance (divide the answer to question 3 into the answer to question 2): _____

7. How many spaces do we need to add? _____
   If the answer to question 6 is larger than the answer to question 5, more spaces are needed. If the answer to question 5 is larger than the answer to question 6, no more spaces are needed. (Remember: This is an immediate need and does not consider future growth.)

*8. I have a problem finding a parking space on Sunday morning. (7.28) _____
   If so, what hour do I arrive? _____

Growth Principle 14: Growth Can Occur Even Though the Church Cannot Afford to Build

1. If we plan or need to build, how much is the approximate yearly debt service on the new facility we will need to build? _____

2. What percent of our budget would this be? _____

3. Our total indebtedness is: _____

4. The percent of our present debt service to our budget is (find this amount in Growth Principle 17, question 24): _____

5. The percent of our debt service to budget with a new facility added will be (add question 2 and question 4): _____

6. When was the last building program? _____

7. What was built? _____

Growth Principle 15: Growth Can Occur without Merely Transferring Members from One Church to Another

1. Breakdown of new members for the past ten years (list most current year first):

Year	Profession of Faith	Other Denomination	Same Denomination	Total
TOTALS:				

2. Does column one outnumber columns two and three? _____

3. Do we intentionally reach out to the unchurched? _____
   If yes, describe how on a separate piece of paper.

   Answers to questions 4 through 6 are taken from the four-week survey in worship.

4. What is the average number of miles our members drive to work? _____

5. What is the average number of minutes our members drive to work? _____

6. What is the average number of miles our members drive to church? _____

   (If the answer to question 4 is larger than the answer to question 6, concentrate on meeting the needs of the people represented in those miles.)

   Answers to questions 7, 8, 10, and 12 can be obtained through the Chamber of Commerce or Percept. However, we strongly suggest that you obtain a Percept Demographic Study of your area. We recommend you order only the Map and the free transparencies of your choice. If you supply the Percept Demographic Study with the Ministry Audit, you do not need to fill out questions 7, 8, and 9.

7. How many people live within a ten-mile radius of the church? _____
   Sixty percent of these are unchurched prospects.

8. Who are these unchurched people?
   Singles, never married _____
   Single-parent families _____
   Singles, divorced _____

Young families _____
Older families _____
Middle-aged families _____
Senior citizens _____
Ethnic minorities _____
Others _____

9. Which group is not being adequately ministered to in our area?
   (Call the churches in your area and inquire what programs they offer.)

   _____

   _____

   _____

   _____

10. Has the population of our county increased or decreased over the last ten years? _____
    By how much? _____

11. Has our church kept pace with the population increase/decrease of our county? _____

12. Are the schools full in our area? _____

Growth Principle 16: Growth Almost Always Occurs if the Congregation Is Friendly toward Visitors

1. How many dollars and what percent of our budget do we spend on the following forms of advertising?

Yellow Pages	$ _____	Newspaper	$ _____
Flyers	$ _____	Radio	$ _____
Television	$ _____	Direct Mail	$ _____
Other	$ _____		
TOTAL	$ _____		
PERCENT OF OUR BUDGET	_____%		

   Does the total amount represent 5 percent of our budget? _____

2. How many new families visit each week? _____
   a. Do we contact them within forty-eight hours? _____
   b. If so, who makes the contact?

   _____

   _____

   _____

   _____

   _____

3. What percent of these families join our church? _____
   (Multiply question 2 by 52 and divide the number into the number of new families that join each year.)

4. What brought these families to our church?
   Friends and relatives _____
   Driving by _____
   Newspaper _____
   Yellow Pages _____
   Preschool _____
   Singles' groups _____
   Television _____
   Banner _____
   Direct Mail _____
   Other _____

5. How many contacts are made each week with unchurched people? _____

6. Does someone on our staff work on behalf of the unchurched twenty hours each week? _____

7. Do we make it clear in worship that we expect visitors each Sunday? _____
   Does our bulletin reflect this? _____

*8. All of our ministries have an outreach component to them that is an entry point into the life of the congregation. (4.80) _____

9. How many visitors are on our mailing list each week? _____

10. Do we put visitors on the mailing list the first time they visit? _____

*11. We have adequate exterior and interior signs posted around the church. (3.84) _____

*12. We have an adequate number of trained hosts and hostesses. (4.95) _____

13. How do we collect the names of first-time visitors?

_____

_____

_____

_____

14. Do we designate 10 percent of our parking spaces for visitors? _____

*15. When at church, members go out of their way to meet and welcome people they do not know. (3.99) _____

*16. Our members pray regularly that the church will grow spiritually and numerically. (4.26) _____

17. Do we provide information packets for visitors? _____

18. Do we have a booth or designated area for information? _____
    If so, is it well marked? _____

19. Do we have a decision booth where people can register any spiritual decision made during worship and receive help? _____

20. Is a sizable portion of our budget designed to help our leaders connect with the outside world? _____

Growth Principle 17: Asking for Money Encourages Growth

1. List budget totals for the past ten years, including operational expense and debt service (list the most recent year first):

Year	Budget Total

*2. Our church talks often about money and financial stewardship. (3.94) _____

*3. We avoid telling people the church needs their money and instead talk about people's need to become stewards. (4.50) _____

4. Do we have a pledge drive every year for the budget? _____
   If not, do we systematically teach tithing as a spiritual discipline? _____
   If we do not use a pledge drive, what material do we use to teach tithing?

_____

_____

_____

_____

   If you do not have a pledge drive, ignore all of the following questions about pledging.

5. What time of the year is the pledge drive? _____

6. Do we have at least three weeks of education prior to taking pledges? _____

7. Does our pledge card ask only for money? _____

*8. Our lead pastor plays the following role in the pledge drive:

_____

_____

_____

_____

9. List the number and average of pledges for each of the past five years (list most recent year first):

Year	Number of Pledges	Average Amount	Total Pledged	Budget	Percentage of Budget

10. Do our pledges underwrite no more than 70 to 90 percent of our budget?

11. Has the amount and the number of pledges increased or decreased each year? _____

12. Based on our records, what kind of income can we expect next year if we do nothing different?

Pledges/current members	_____
Pledges/new members†	_____
Loose plate	_____
Regular nonpledger	_____
Building usage fees	_____
Foundation	_____
Special offerings	_____
Sunday school offerings	_____
Interest	_____
Memorials	_____
Other	_____
TOTAL	_____

13. Do we select our stewardship leaders based on their giving patterns and willingness to give of themselves? _____

14. Do we contact new members for a pledge? _____

15. Do we keep detailed records of giving and pledge patterns and analyze them regularly? _____

† If you discount your total pledges to reflect your historical pledge loss, then count your anticipated pledge from new members after you have divided them by two. If you do not discount the total pledges from current members, then do not count anticipated pledges from new members.

16. Is our pledge program centered around tithing? _____

17. How are campaigns conducted?

_____

_____

_____

_____

18. Describe the last three stewardship programs:

_____

_____

_____

_____

19. Do we encourage designated giving and discourage a unified budget? _____

20. Do we have regular special offerings for items within the budget? _____

21. Complete the following chart for the last ten years (most recent year first):

Year	Average Worship Attendance	Percent of Income to Average Worship Attendance[†]

22. Does our total budget income (operating and building) equal or exceed $1,000 for every person in worship on an average Sunday? (See above list.) _____

23. Does one-third of our church's income come from no more than one-fourth of our pledges? _____

[†] Divide worship total into income total for each year.

24. Complete the following chart on indebtedness for the last ten years (most recent year first):

Year	Total Debt	Total Percent of Debt to Budget[†]	Budgeted Debt Service (mortgage)	Percent of Debt Service to Budget[††]

25. Is our debt service less than 25 percent of our total operating budget? (See above list.) _____

26. List of financial resources:

    Endowments   _____
    Wills   _____
    Capital Fund Pledges _____
    Cash Reserves   _____
    Foundation   _____
    Stocks and Bonds   _____
    Other   _____
    TOTAL   _____

27. Is there a plan to use this money? _____
    If so, what is it?

_____

_____

_____

_____

28. When was the last capital fund drive? _____

29. Does our lead pastor or someone on the paid staff know what each member gives? _____

[†]To compute percent of indebtedness to budget, divide budget total into indebtedness total for each year.
[††]To compute percent of debt service to budget, divide budget total into budgeted debt service total for each year.

Growth Principle 18: Regular Strategic Mapping Must Be Done for Growth to Be Healthy

1. Does our church have a mission statement that is clear, concise, and open-ended? _____
   If so, what is it?

---

2. Do we have a master plan for the use of land and facilities? _____

*3. Our church's main strength is (list only one):

---

*4. Our church's main weakness is (list only one):

---

*5. The objectives of our pastor and the church match. (2.65) _____

6. List present officially adopted objectives (goals) of the church:

Growth Principle 19: It Takes More Effort to Implement Change Than to Maintain the Status Quo or to Exercise Veto Power

*1. Our church is free from power cliques. (6.20) _____

*2. One or two people derail things that the majority wants. (6.38) _____

*3. The average age of the person filling out this report is: (52) _____

*4. The average length of time the person filling out this report has been a member of this church is (18): _____

5. How many people received the Official Body Survey? _____

6. How many people completed the Official Body Survey? _____

7. Do you make any changes in your schedule in the summer?
   If so, what are they?

   _____

   _____

   _____

   _____

18. I am currently in a small group. _____

19. I am currently serving in the church. _____

10. I have access to electronic mail. _____

Readiness Survey: Staff Total Sheet

1. The nursery should be extra clean, neat, staffed with paid help, and open every time there is a church function.
   Average of responses _____

2. Turf issues are harmful to the growth of a church.
   Average of responses _____

3. I am willing for the facilities to be used, even if they get dirty.
   Average of responses _____

4. Reaching out to new members is just as important as taking care of the present members.
   Average of responses _____

5. I am comfortable with radical change if it will help my church reach more people for Christ.
   Average of responses _____

6. I am seldom concerned about procedure.
   Average of responses _____

7. Paying off the debt is not a major concern to me.
   Average of responses _____

8. I support the idea of spending some of the church savings in order to hire more staff or start new programs.
   Average of responses _____

9. Several worship services are fine with me because I am more interested in meeting the needs of all the people than I am in knowing everyone at church.
   Average of responses _____

10. I am not at all offended when my lead pastor does not give me regular personal attention.
    Average of responses _____

11. I realize that more staff is needed today than in the past.
    Average of responses _____

12. I always trust and affirm my lead pastor's efforts to reach more people for Christ.
    Average of responses _____

Readiness Survey: Official Body Total Sheet

1. The nursery should be extra clean, neat, staffed with paid help, and open every time there is a church function.
   Average of responses _____

2. Turf issues are harmful to the growth of a church.
   Average of responses _____

3. I am willing for the facilities to be used, even if they get dirty.
   Average of responses _____

4. Reaching out to new members is just as important as taking care of the present members.
   Average of responses _____

5. I am comfortable with radical change if it will help my church reach more people for Christ.
   Average of responses _____

6. I am seldom concerned about procedure.
   Average of responses _____

7. Paying off the debt is not a major concern to me.
   Average of responses _____

8. I support the idea of spending some of the church savings in order to hire more staff or start new programs.
   Average of responses _____

9. Several worship services are fine with me because I am more interested in meeting the needs of all the people than I am in knowing everyone at church.
   Average of responses _____

10. I am not at all offended when my lead pastor does not give me regular personal attention.
    Average of responses _____

11. I realize that more staff is needed today than in the past.
    Average of responses _____

12. I always trust and affirm my lead pastor's efforts to reach more people for Christ.
    Average of responses _____

Permission Giving Survey: Official Body Total Sheet

1. Our church leaders believe that people doing the actual ministry should make the majority of the decisions that affect how they do their ministry.
   Average of responses _____

2. People at the lowest level of organization in our church should be able to suggest and implement improvements to their own ministry without going through several committees and levels of approval.
   Average of responses _____

3. All persons in the congregation should be free to live out their spiritual gifts in the congregation without getting approval, even if it means starting a new ministry.
   Average of responses _____

4. The nature of ministry lends itself to a team-based approach rather than to individual effort.
   Average of responses _____

5. Our leadership is flexible enough to permit restructuring or reorganization so that the organization facilitates the new mission of the church.
   Average of responses _____

6. It is possible to organize ministry so that teams can take responsibility for entire ministries.
   Average of responses _____

7. There is enough complexity in our ministry to allow for initiative and decision making.
   Average of responses _____

8. Our leadership is comfortable with individuals or teams making autonomous, on-the-spot decisions.
   Average of responses _____

9. The laity are interested in or willing to organize into teams or small groups.
   Average of responses _____

10. Our key leadership is willing to share its power with those who are not in leadership.
    Average of responses _____

11. Our church has a history of following through on new ideas.
    Average of responses _____

12. Our key lay leadership is willing to radically change its own roles and behavior.
    Average of responses _____

13. Our church is secure enough to guarantee a period of relative stability during which permission giving can develop.
    Average of responses _____

14. We have adequate resources to support and train our people.
    Average of responses _____

15. Our staff and key lay leadership understand that becoming a permission-giving church is a lengthy, time-consuming, and labor-intensive process that may take five years, and are willing to make the investment in time.
    Average of responses _____

16. Our church has a network that could provide information to any layperson anytime.
    Average of responses _____

17. Our laypeople have the skills needed to take greater responsibility for the ministries of the church.
    Average of responses _____

18. Our senior lead pastor is willing to invest in training the team leaders.
    Average of responses _____

19. Our finance and trustee committees should exist to serve the needs of those trying to implement ministry.
    Average of responses _____

20. Our leaders are more concerned with discovering ways to reach the unchurched than with how those ministries are discovered or implemented.
    Average of responses _____

Permission Giving Survey: Staff Total Sheet

1. Our church leaders believe that people doing the actual ministry should make the majority of the decisions that affect how they do their ministry.
   Average of responses _____

2. People at the lowest level of organization in our church should be able to suggest and implement improvements to their own ministry without going through several committees and levels of approval.
   Average of responses _____

3. All persons in the congregation should be free to live out their spiritual gifts in the congregation without getting approval, even if it means starting a new ministry.
   Average of responses _____

4. The nature of ministry lends itself to a team-based approach rather than to individual effort.
   Average of responses _____

5. Our leadership is flexible enough to permit restructuring or reorganization so that the organization facilitates the new mission of the church.
   Average of responses _____

6. It is possible to organize ministry so that teams can take responsibility for entire ministries.
   Average of responses _____

7. There is enough complexity in our ministry to allow for initiative and decision making.
   Average of responses _____

8. Our leadership is comfortable with individuals or teams making autonomous, on-the-spot decisions.
   Average of responses _____

9. The laity are interested in or willing to organize into teams or small groups.
   Average of responses _____

10. Our key leadership is willing to share its power with those who are not in leadership.
    Average of responses _____

11. Our church has a history of following through on new ideas.
    Average of responses _____

12. Our key lay leadership is willing to radically change its own roles and behavior.
    Average of responses _____

13. Our church is secure enough to guarantee a period of relative stability during which permission giving can develop.
    Average of responses _____

14. We have adequate resources to support and train our people.
    Average of responses _____

15. Our staff and key lay leadership understand that becoming a permission-giving church is a lengthy, time-consuming, and labor-intensive process that may take five years and are willing to make the investment in time.
    Average of responses _____

16. Our church has a network that could provide information to any layperson anytime.
    Average of responses _____

17. Our laypeople have the skills needed to take greater responsibility for the ministries of the church.
    Average of responses _____

18. Our senior lead pastor is willing to invest in training the team leaders.
    Average of responses _____

19. Our finance and trustee committees should exist to serve the needs of those trying to implement ministry.
    Average of responses _____

20. Our leaders are more concerned with discovering ways to reach the unchurched than with how those ministries are discovered or implemented.
    Average of responses _____

SECTION FIVE

THE STUDY GUIDE

The Basic Law of Congregational Life

You will be my witnesses in Jerusalem, in all Judea and Samaria, and to the ends of the earth. (Acts 1:8 b)

> Churches grow when they intentionally reach out to people instead of concentrating on their institutional needs. Churches die when they concentrate on their own needs.
> This is the Basic Law of Congregational Life.

As a young boy, I was fascinated by the effect of throwing pebbles into a pond. One tiny pebble would produce an ever-widening circle that eventually filled the entire pond, and if I had thrown the stone near the center of the pond, when the ripple reached the bank it rippled back to the point where it had originated.

The church of Jesus Christ is like an ever-widening circle. As it gives itself away on behalf of others, it grows. Everything we do on behalf of others comes back to us. This is the way life works. We give and we receive.

One week, after preaching a sermon entitled "The Ever-widening Circle," I received a note from a member of the church: "It's time for some sermons about personal and spiritual growth as well as institutional growth. We have some needs out here, too!"

The member missed the point of the sermon. Churches are healthiest when they reach out. Members are best nurtured when they nurture others. The art of giving has healing effects. Jesus taught us this in all he said and did: those who lose their lives will find them (Matt. 10:39). We have a need to help others. God made us that way. We find emotional and spiritual health by moving beyond concern for self.

The Biblical Basis

The Bible is filled with references to the Basic Law of Congregational Life, such as "love your neighbor as yourself" (Matt. 22:39). The most gripping reference may be when Jesus talked about this law in the commission that he left with his disciples in the upper room. He instructed them in the law when he said, "You will be my witnesses in Jerusalem, in all Judea and Samaria, and to the ends of the earth" (Acts 1:8b). Our Lord's last words are very clear—the mission of the church is to continually increase its ability to give itself away on behalf of all God's creation.

Examine the diagram of the ever-widening circle. The circles represent the biblical life cycle of a church. It is the biblical affirmation that the farther a congregation moves from the center, the healthier the church becomes. The less of "you" and the more of God there is at the center of the circle, the healthier the congregation becomes.

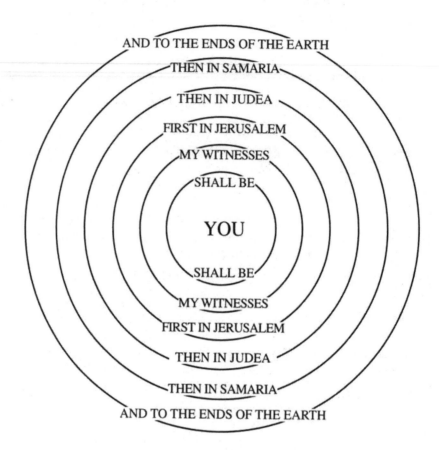

The third ring, "Jerusalem," represents a local congregation. One of the more common excuses given by both clergy and laity for avoiding making disciples is that churches should take better care of their present members before reaching out for more. But life doesn't work that way. The best way to nurture your members is for them to reach out to nurture someone else.

The fourth ring, "Judea," represents the geographic area that surrounds a local church. Every local church must feel a responsibility for an area larger than its own parish. The larger the area, the healthier the church will be.

The next ring, "Samaria," represents the unloved and unwanted people of our society. The Samaritans were the outcasts of Jesus' day, but Jesus said that the churches must reach out to include the present-day Samaritans.

The sixth ring, "the ends of the earth," represents world missions. A local church needs a vision for world missions that does not place a limit on its sphere of responsibility. For church growth with integrity, a church must really believe that with God's help, there are no limits to the scope of its ministry. The circle always must be growing wider.

The Argument

The Basic Law of Congregational Life is the basis for biblical ministry because it focuses on life's fundamental challenge: to overcome self-centeredness. Jesus asked us to be his witnesses, not our own. He asked us to move away from considering ourselves the center of our universe, to put others in our place. He knew that when we do so, we become healthy.

One Sunday after worship I received an anonymous note scribbled on the back of a registration card: "Who says our church has to grow? I think [our church] has grown enough." On another occasion, when I announced a series of sermons on the ever-widening circle, I received this note: "Please make it clear at the beginning that growth for growth's sake is not what you're talking about." At another time I was handed one that read: "I hope we're not trying to reach more new members just to fund the budget."

In most churches, reaching out to non-Christians and unchurched people is almost as difficult to talk about as money or politics. Why? Probably because we do not want to lose control of our own church; new people mean less control for ourselves. We are comfortable the way we are, and we do not like to change to accommodate new people and new ideas.

The Basic Law of Congregational Life is a reminder that life does not revolve around self. As a rule, twenty-first–century Christians have not understood that life centers around our relationship with Christ and others, not around ourselves. We have viewed the mission of the church primarily in light of our own personal needs. We have failed to understand that we are made in such a way that our needs are nurtured best as we take care of the needs of others. When we talk about taking care of our own membership before being involved in evangelism or outreach, we reveal a lack of understanding of the mission of the church. The basic mission of the church is to help me nurture others; and in that process, I will be nurtured too!

Why Do Churches Grow and Die?

Allow me to introduce Joe. Joe has been married for ten years. He and his wife have two children: one is six years of age; the other, three months. Neither Joe nor his wife has been to church since they left their parents' homes. The older child is now ready to start school, and Joe's wife has decided it is also time for the children to receive a Christian education. Joe doesn't want to go to church, but he gives in because his wife insists.

The first obstacle Joe faces is a lack of convenient parking. By the time he gets to the church, he is irritated because he has had to walk a block. The second obstacle is the absence of directional signs to the nursery. No member of the church is willing to break away from a personal conversation to help Joe's family find their way. By now Joe is fuming.

Finally, Joe's family locates the sanctuary, only to sit shoulder-to-shoulder with a lot of strangers. Joe does not like to have strangers that close. He wants plenty of elbow room. As the service progresses, Joe is asked to hold up his hand so that everyone will know he is not a member. He does not want anyone to know he is there, much less that he is not a member.

Then without warning, the whole congregation suddenly rises and begins to sing something that all good Christians are supposed to know—the Doxology. Joe doesn't know the Doxology. The page number is printed in the bulletin, so he frantically finds the right place, only to realize that the song is over.

The sermon puts Joe to sleep because it talks about things he cannot apply to his daily life and it uses words with which he is not familiar. When the service is over, Joe and his family leave without being greeted by anyone. Later, Joe informs his wife that he does not intend to go through that torture again!

Now allow me to introduce Max. Max is a long-term member of the church Joe just visited. His children are all grown. He is a few years from retirement, and he has helped the church with several building programs. Max has been a member for so long he can't remember what it's like to be uncommitted to Christ and his church.

When told about Joe's reaction to his visit to the church, Max said, "If he isn't any more committed than that, let him stay at home. I don't mind walking a block to church. Besides, he's probably not willing to help pay for a new sanctuary anyway."

Christian churches are filled with good people like Max, and because of that, they are dying. Dying churches fail to remember that many of their present members were once just like Joe. They were not committed, and they could not have cared less about attending church. On the other hand, today's world is filled with people like Joe—good people with families, but unchurched and uncommitted.

There is a world of difference between the value systems of Max and Joe. Max believes people should be as far out of debt as possible; Joe thinks the more credit he has, the more affluent he is. Max trusts institutions; Joe doesn't. Max serves God out of duty, obligation, and commitment; Joe serves out of compassion. Max has long-term plans and goals; Joe prefers instant gratification. Max married for life; Joe married in the hope that it would last. Max grew up in church; Joe did not. For growth to occur in mainline Protestant churches, Max must recognize the difference between his world and Joe's world.

Integrity Factors in a Biblical Church

Because there is always the danger that numbers and quantity can take precedence over a concern for people, any discussion about the growth of a church must include enough integrity factors to avoid the possibility that quantity will become the primary emphasis of ministry. There are at least seven integrity factors present in healthy church growth:

1. People take precedence over institutional maintenance.
2. Jesus is always the center of the message.
3. Ministry is balanced.
4. There is a high ratio between the membership and the number of people who attend worship.
5. There is a balance between money spent on the church and money spent on others.
6. A higher percentage of members join by profession of faith and restoration of vows than by transfer of membership.
7. An inclusive faith is stressed.

These seven factors are examined throughout this book along with the basic ingredients in a faithful, biblical church, which are:

- Being biblically grounded
- Maintaining cultural relevance
- Existing to transform lives of both Christian and non-Christian
- Equipping and mobilizing the congregation
- Establishing a community built on trust
- Structuring your church to grow disciples

The Basic Law of Congregational Life is that churches are healthiest when they reach out to others. Churches grow because they are intentionally concerned about the needs of others. Churches die because they concentrate primarily on their internal needs. With this law before us, we are now ready to explore how the growth principles affect our congregations.

Growth Principles 1 through 6: Growing People, Making Disciples

Growth Principle 1: Growth Is Not Concerned with Numbers but with Growing Disciples (Key Questions: 1, 2, 4–5, 6, 7, 8, 10)

Data Source: Worship Survey; Staff Survey, questions 1-7; Official Body Survey Totals Spreadsheet "D:\Spreadsheets\Body Survey-Totals Spreadsheet.xls," questions 1-3.

Question 1: What is the age, sex, and marital status of adult worshippers?

The information for answering question 1 comes from the Worship Survey that you took on four consecutive Sundays. When figuring average attendance, count the children who are present even if they do not attend worship. Just count the average number of children in Sunday school and add that to the worship average. If you are using the spreadsheet file from the bonus CD-ROM, retrieve The Worship Survey Totals Spreadsheet (D:\Spreadsheets\Worship Survey-Totals Spreadsheet.xls) and print a report, so that you can port the data to the Ministry Audit.

The Four Generations

The ages are broken down into the four key generations as described by William Straus and Neil Howe in their book *Generations: The History of America's Future*. They explore the cycle of generations in American history. They are the G.I. generation, the silent generation, the baby boom generation, the baby buster generation, and the millennial generation. By studying these generations, a church can decide where to place its emphases.

People born from 1900 to 1924 make up the *G.I. generation*. The G.I. generation made up 7.3 percent of the national population in 1998. They made unprecedented progress in science, medicine, and the pursuit of individual liberties around the globe, especially as they overcame the tyranny and evil of two global wars that were sandwiched around a massive economic depression. Now this generation feels that its values and achievements are under attack.

The challenge the church faces is how to help this generation surrender some of its hard-earned privileges for the good of others and the future. Faced with uncertainty about health and longevity, this group will now begin to deal with the fact that they no longer have a future that is more promising than the past, and the future they now see may be filled with uncertainty and threats. The act of losing their lives that they may find them will be a practical issue as they experience the loss of power and control over their lives, society, and the church.

People born from 1925 to 1945 make up the *silent generation.* The silent generation made up 12.7 percent of the national population in 1998. They feel caught between the G.I. generation and the baby boom generation. They seek to find compromise, trying to balance the needs of aging parents and boomer children who have turned away from the values of their grandparents. Their inclination to find a middle ground between the two groups will not be appreciated by either group. They served as leaders in the 1990s, but this leadership was short, as society and the church made the shift to baby boom–generation leaders. The church must work hard to keep this age group in order to have the benefits of its sense of fairness and compassion. This will not happen without effort on the church's part. The church will need to be sure that it is keeping some members of the silent generation in leadership positions.

People born from 1946 to 1964 make up the *baby boom generation.* This generation made up 24.1 percent of the national population in 1998. The boom generation gets attention. Its size makes it a key group for any congregation that is seeking to plan its future. This group is not easy to work with as they turn their attention to reform the institutions in which they are members. The church is no exception. Women are seeking leadership and are not satisfied to play a secondary role. The church needs to focus on societal issues. Abortion is one of the key issues, and boomers are on both sides and hold uncompromisingly to positions that are difficult to reconcile.

Spiritual growth issues remain high on their agenda. While family issues are important to them, families are more diverse than anytime before. This generation sees the fading of early retirement from their plans. They are a healthier generation, and as their children grow up and move from home, boomers are traveling and continuing to seek experiences for growth. They want experiences that make a contribution not only to others but to their own growth as well. They now need help dealing with aging parents while rearing families that were begun later in life. They feel tension between these two responsibilities. Day care services for the parents of the boomers are beginning to be as important as day care for their children was in years past. Many of the women in this generation are charting untested waters and have little hope for help from the silent and G.I. generations. Women's concerns are becoming more important.

This generation is looking for ways to recapture the collective experiences of their youth, and as the most educated generation in our history, they are seeking more opportunities to explore their own spiritual and intellectual growth and will *find* them in many novel and new ways. The challenge to the church is to contribute to this generation's maturation, so that they are able to deal with their mortality and discover not only their need for grace but the need to be graceful toward others. It is hard today for a church to grow if it is not reaching baby boomers. Bill Easum's book *How to Reach Baby Boomers* discusses the challenges of that task in detail (see Recommended Reading on our Web site. Simply go to www.easumbandy.com, click Free Resources, then click Library).

People born from 1965 to 1982 make up the *baby buster generation*. The buster generation made up 30.1 percent of the national population in 1998. This generation presents a new challenge. One cannot assume that what has worked with the baby boom generation will work with the baby bust generation. Members of this generation will live their entire lives in the shadow of the boomers, and are facing a much less promising future than the boomers did at the same age. They are dealing with issues such as AIDS, a sluggish economy, governments having to raise taxes and cut benefits, and the elimination of many good blue- and white-collar jobs. Realism rather than idealism will be the mainstay of their lives. Practical concerns will remain important to them. They will need help to confront the harsh realities that they will face their entire lives. They will be pragmatic, and this will be an important balance for the idealism of the boomers. The church must now begin to focus serious attention on the busters.

"Twentysomething" adults are the primary target for church growth over the next thirty years. They will be even more important than baby boomers. The journey from the age of eighteen into the thirties is a turbulent time of transition. Times of transition are the best times to reach people. However, many of this generation will have no church background, and thus they may not turn to the church in times of trouble. It is essential that the church find ways to reach out to them.

People born from 1983 to 2003 make up the *millennial generation*. The millennial generation made up 25.4 percent of the population in 1998. We have already seen the first signs of interest in providing this generation with the best quality education, and that includes providing places of safety for learning in an increasingly violent world. There are also signs everywhere acknowledging that the needs of children have been ignored. Members of this generation will be rational doers, and the educational and emotional training we give them will steer them in that direction. The 1990s was the decade for any and all programs for children and youth, and this trend continues in the first years of the new century. It will pose important challenges to the church.

Interpreting the Worship Survey

With question 1 of the Ministry Audit, you will be calculating the adult percentages that are based on the Worship Survey. The following steps explain how to fill in the blanks. Keep in mind that the statistics represent only the adult population in worship.

1. M/M = male married; M/S = male single; F/M = female married; F/S = female single. Calculate the percentages of respondents who fall within
   a. the four main age groups;
   b. the sixteen categories.

> Hint: Add the percentages for the G.I. generation and the silent generation. The lower the combined percentage for these two categories, the better. If more than 50 percent of the worshipping congregation is over fifty years of age, it is more difficult for the congregation to reach the unchurched because of the resistance to change. The higher this percentage, the more urgent it is that you act strategically.
>
> In 2005, people fifty years of age have a life expectancy of 29.1 more years.

2. In the far-right column under question 1, note the gender and marital status of all the respondents to the Worship Survey.

> Hint: On average, males make up 48 percent of attendees at churches in the United States. If the proportion of males attending your church falls significantly below 38 percent, consider developing ministries for men.

3. You can approximate the number of singles, separated, and divorced people in worship by counting the number of M/S and F/S people born between 1943 and 1961. Singles born between those years are more likely to be single, separated, or divorced—not widowed.

Question 2: Does our pastor understand the everyday world of our members?

This is the most complicated question and deserves your special attention. The score comes from the Official Body Survey (D:\Spreadsheets\Body Survey-Totals Spreadsheet.xls) on the CD-ROM, question 1. This question is important because the lead pastor must have a good image throughout the leadership before significant transformation or growth can occur.

There are several ways to interpret this question. For example, a negative score could mean that the pastor isn't competent, isn't liked, or is pushing the church too hard. Or it could mean that the lay leaders themselves are conflicted. Also, remember to see the big picture. This question alone may not give the whole picture so you need to look several other places to test what a negative score here might mean. So if you get a negative answer here you might do the following.

- Compare this answer with the leadership's answers to the questions about the pastor in Growth Principle 7, questions 5 through 8; and Growth Principle 9, questions 2 and 6 through 16. If the majority of these scores are positive (low), you don't have a problem. If the majority of these scores are negative (high), you may have a problem.
- However, before you panic, turn to Growth Principle 11 and see if the scores on questions 3 through 17 are negative or positive. If negative (high), then the odds are you have a conflicted or unhappy group of lay leaders and the scores regarding the pastor are unreliable. If these scores are positive (low), then a problem exists between the pastor and the lay leaders. What the problem is may not be evident but it needs to be resolved.
- Usually, the longer a pastor has been at a church, the lower and more positive the scores. Smaller churches that have had a high rate of pastoral turnover in recent years usually score higher than average (2.73).

Question 4: Has there been any major controversy or division in the preceding five years?

The most common conflicts I have encountered are (1) the adult choir does not cooperate, (2) the trustees exert far too much power in the decision-making process,

(3) the finance committee or the financial secretary makes life miserable for anyone wanting to start a new ministry that costs money, and (4) there are one or two long-term members of the church who have no office in the church but must be consulted before any decision can be made. Has the congregation settled and resolved the conflicts? Unresolved corporate pain is one of the top ten reasons why churches do not reach the unchurched. If serious conflict from the past still haunts your congregation, resolve the conflict before attempting any of the recommendations you might make as a result of this audit. The number one thing non-Christians need when they attend church is an environment of trust and community.

Question 5: Does our church deal openly with controversy?

As you can see from the average score, it is not unusual for a significant number of people to feel as if their church does not deal openly with conflict. This often means that there are people in the church who feel stifled. Perhaps they have had new ideas turned down.

Questions 6, 7, 8, 10: How do we make decisions?

All four questions deal with aspects of the same issue. The goal is to have as flat an organization as possible and to make the decision-making process open and accessible to anyone. Are there several layers of administration? Are numerous meetings required before a decision can be made? Are most of the decisions on new proposals "NO"? If so, these are signs of decay and too much structure. For more help in this area, see Bill Easum's book *Unfreezing Moves,* published by Abingdon Press.

Hint: In question 8 of the Ministry Audit (the answer comes from the Staff Survey [D:\Spreadsheets\Staff.doc on the CD-ROM], question 5), look for comments such as "trustees" or "one or two people." The most effective churches have no more than one level of withholding permission. People should be able to start new ministries by approaching one central committee that can give an answer, rather than having to go through a labyrinth of committees. For more information on permission-giving organizations, see Bill Easum's book *Sacred Cows Make Gourmet Burgers,* published by Abingdon Press.

Action Items for Growing Disciples

1. If more than 50 percent of the worshippers in your church were born before 1942, begin new ministries specifically for young adults. The demographics, the resources suggested at www.easumbandy.com, as well as your knowledge of the community can guide you in the process.
2. Resolve any major conflict before attempting to start new ministries, unless the new ministries are the only way to resolve or do away with the conflict. Failure to do this has caused many churches to fail in this process.
3. Consider restructuring only if you have a lot of red tape or several layers of groups who withhold permission for new ministries. Don't worry with restructuring unless it is absolutely impossible to get around or through it. Restructuring works only in a healthy church. But remember that restructuring does not help a church unless that church has vision and is willing to act on a plan.

4. If you simply can't afford a Percept Demographic Report, call the Chamber of Commerce and tell them you are a pastor or church leader trying to find out more about your community. Ask if they can send you any demographic information they have concerning the population, projects, trends, age, gender, income, working habits, or any other social, religious, or economic issue in your area.

Growth Principle 2: Growth Occurs When People Are Given a Wide Variety of Choices (questions 1 through 8, and 11 through 15)

Data Source: Staff Survey ("D:\Surveys\Staff\Staff.doc"), questions 8 through 25.

Question 1: Does our church offer a balanced ministry?

One of the key features of the last part of the twentieth century was providing a wide variety of high-quality choices. The more quality choices a church can provide for both churched and unchurched people, the healthier the church will be.

Balance is the key. Churches that are committed to social justice have ministries that approach pain and injustice in two ways: (1) through social justice ministries, such as Habitat for Humanity, clothes closets, and homeless shelters, that address immediate needs; and (2) the root-cause ministries, such as action groups that organize people to change the way economic decisions are made in one's community or state. Churches need more high-quality ministries in the mercy category than in the categories of love and justice combined, because more people are unchurched today than are churched.

Questions 2, 3, 4.: Does our church offer weekday ministries for children?

A childcare program, run by the church as an extension of its children's ministry, provides a needed service, teaches values, and evangelizes as well.

Weekday ministries for children, including preschool, day care, Parent's Day Out, Parent's Night Out, kindergarten, or grade school, work best for the children, the parents, and the church if the ministries are considered an extension of the church. It is best if the person responsible for the ministries is part of the church staff and is accountable either to the pastor or to the person who gives regular supervision of the church staff. The weekday children's ministries and the Sunday school need to work closely together so that most toys and equipment can be used by both. The budget needs to be set by the official body of the church and the curriculum needs to include religious training and offer chapel once a week. In most cases the ministries should not only be totally self-sustaining but should also return some percent of their gross income to the church budget to help with other ministries that cannot sustain themselves, such as the children's Sunday school or a singles' ministry.

This program is so basic that it is worth designing the building program around it, keeping in mind that you will need to use these facilities twenty years from now for elder care weekday ministries.

Question 6: Does our church have adult day care?

Adult day care is needed more each year because the United States is graying at a fairly rapid pace. Although it is not as strong a need now as day care for children, the need is growing and will continue to do so. This should be kept in mind if you are thinking of building in the next few years.

Questions 7, 12: How often do we start new Sunday school classes?

Sunday school classes more than six months old tend to be hard for new people to join. It's not that the classes are unfriendly, but that they have become close-knit families, and families do not take in new members easily. If you are a program-based church and are interested in cutting the inactive list, then establish new classes every six months. If you decide to develop a small-group ministry around the "meta" model, you do not have to worry about starting new classes. For ideas on how to start new classes, see some of the resources listed on our Web site under "Sunday school." Simply go to www.easumbandy.com and click Free Resources and then FAQs.

Question 8: How many adults attend Sunday school, in how many classes?

Equipping adults is the most important ministry in the church. Adults bring children; children seldom bring adults. Skill training is the most challenging adult ministry today. It is increasingly common for adults to lack skills in such basic areas as parenting, social graces, making friends, and interpersonal relations. Most adults today know very little about the Bible. Until they do, it is very unlikely that serious ministry will occur. There are several Bible studies that can begin the process of educating adults about the Bible (see "Bible Studies-Print Resources"; simply go to www.easumbandy.com and click Free Resources and then FAQs).

The best Sunday school classes are small-group Bible studies with a focus on outreach and assimilation. Keep these classes small by starting a new class every time the class attendance averages fifteen or twenty, even if it means there will be more than one class for some age groups. Large classes are good for singles and for those born before 1950. Ask each class to set a goal of 5 to 15 percent growth and to report the percentages to the person in charge of Sunday school. Ask the Sunday school class to appoint a shepherd to call all of the first-time visitors. Consider using conference calls for Sunday school classes that wish to talk with a member of the class who has been absent or who is having a special day such as a birthday.

Question 10: How many youth attend Sunday school, in how many classes?

It is essential to have Sunday school classes for youth if you are a program-based church. If you are a nontraditional church, youth ministry may occur Sunday evening or during the week. The best youth ministries today include mentoring, small groups, and youth-led worship designed for youth. Fellowship is also important but not nearly so much as in the past.

It does not work well to combine junior-high youth and senior-high youth. At this point in their lives, they are years apart in their interests. The only exception here is when some churches use the more mature seniors to lead and mentor the lower-junior-high grades.

Church leaders should get to know the youth in the church by name and provide mentoring opportunities for them. Do the leaders stop in the hallways to talk with the youth? Do the youth have any say in the affairs of the church? Parents should be involved in the youth program instead of having the youth worker simply taking care of the youth. If you have a youth worker, that person should understand that he or she is working primarily with families who have youth and not just the youth.

Church leaders should provide a positive vision for the youth. This is helped by the amount of good space given to the youth. Do they have their own room that they can decorate? Do they have enough space for more than just sitting around in a circle to hear a lesson? How much money is in the budget for the youth? Are retreats and outings planned? Is there a regular trip planned each year open only to those who have been in worship, Sunday school, and any evening youth program on three out of four Sundays? And do the youth have to raise most of the money spent on youth trips?

Youth should never get the leftovers, such as old couches and broken furniture. Their rooms should be some of the best in the church. Facilities should not be better cared for than the youth. The congregation should be concerned more about the youth than about keeping the facilities clean.

The church should have clear-cut policies actively and consistently put into place and lived out by those who work with the youth, on alcohol, drugs, movies shown at the church, adult behavior, and so on. Background checks should be done on all youth workers. Check the resources listed under "Youth." Simply go to www.easumbandy.com and click Free Resources and then FAQs.

Question 11: How many children attend Sunday school, in how many classes?

For traditional churches, it is best to keep all elementary grades separate and even to have a class for children who turned six too late to enroll in school. It is best to have a male and a female teacher. Male teachers can make an important contribution to the lives of children who do not have male role models at home. Most children learn better today through computers than through print. Put three or four computers in the children's Sunday school area and obtain some good Bible software. Arrange a schedule that will allow all the classes to use the computers.

Nontraditional churches are going out of their way to avoid the classroom look. The hallways and entries into the rooms are designed around a theme. Often the teaching is done in a large group using storytelling, music, and video to drive home the theme, followed by small group breaks-outs where the children reflect on what they have learned that morning. Check out "Children" on our Web site. Simply go to www.easumbandy.com and click Free Resources and then FAQs.

To see pictures of how one church designed its children's area so that it didn't look like classrooms, go to http://easumbandy.com/resources/index.php?action=details &record=1149. To see how many churches are changing children's Sunday school, go to http://easumbandy.com/resources/index.php?action=details&record=1333.

Question 14: Does our church have midweek programs?

A major change during the past twenty years has been the increasing demand for seven-day-a-week churches. A healthy, traditional, program-based church will have two to three people on the property during the week for every one person in worship on Sunday. (Read Lyle Schaller's book *The Seven-Day-A-Week Church,* published by Abingdon Press.)

Often churches with fewer than three hundred people in worship fail to develop core ministries. Core ministries are those ministries that are as important to continue as worship and Sunday school. These ministries are carried over from layperson to layperson, clergy to clergy. A core ministry is anything that is considered so important that no matter who the pastor is or what the skill level of the laity is, the program continues. As they grow, program-based churches often fail to expand their number of core ministries that bring new people into a relationship with the church, they stop meeting the needs of people, and they stagnate. Nontraditional churches tend to have fewer but better core ministries that are focused on growing individuals and the Kingdom rather than supporting the church.

In 90 percent of U.S. communities, people between the ages of twenty-eight and forty-five are the largest segment of the population, as well as the largest unchurched adult group. We know several important things about these people:

1. They do not trust institutions and have rejected the institutional church.
2. They are morally adrift but want help finding an anchor for themselves and their children.
3. They resist rules but respond to reason.
4. They have many legitimate questions about faith and Christianity.
5. They want an experience more than values and beliefs.
6. They are not joiners but are looking for a place to belong—a place for relationships.
7. They distrust authority but respond to personal mentoring and role-modeling.
8. They are not loyal to denominations but respond to churches that meet their needs.
9. They are tolerant of others' beliefs but expect their spiritual leaders to know where they stand and what they believe.
10. They may attend church if a friend invites them, but they often do not stay because the worship is boring.
11. They want anonymity.
12. They look for quality.
13. They expect "how-to" and "so what" sermons.
14. They do not like "holier than thou" sermons.

Traditional churches are basically missing these people.

The most helpful thing you can do to determine which new ministries to begin and which ones to drop is to conduct a demographic study of your ministry area. Concentrate on an area five to ten miles around your church. If you do not have access to a Percept demographic report (check under "Demographics" on our Web site; simply go to www.easumbandy.com and click Free Resources and then FAQs), make sure questions 8 and 9 under Growth Principle 15 of the Ministry Audit have been filled out. You can gather demographic information about your area by calling the Chamber of Commerce.

Focus groups can help you determine which new ministries to begin. These groups need to be made up of either very new members (who have been members for no longer than one year) or unchurched people in the neighborhood. See "Focus Groups" on our Web site. Simply go to www.easumbandy.com and click Free Resources and then FAQs.

Question 15: Does our church have Bible studies?

Weekday Bible study is essential today because the unchurched are on a spiritual journey. If the emphasis is on content, Bible study works best when it is done in large groups led by the pastor. If the emphasis is on changing lives, then it is best done in small groups led by laypeople. Both emphases are essential.

Action Items for Giving People Choices

1. Based on your demographic study (if you have one), decide which new outreach ministries to begin, which present ones to strengthen, and which present ones to drop.
2. If you have only one adult class on Sunday, begin a second one.
3. If you have a weekday children's ministry that is not part of your church's ministry and which pays the church for renting the space, find a way to replace it with one that your church runs. Make it distinctively Christian.
4. Take a long look at your children's ministry. Compare it to the pictures on our Web site. If it doesn't measure up, make plans to change the environment. If you are still using only print curriculum, what can you do to insert storytelling, music, and video? For example, take a look at what VeggieTales now offers. Check out this site: http://www.bigidea.com/.

Growth Principle 3: Growth Occurs When People Are Matched with Their Gifts and Skills (Key Questions: 1, 2)

> Data Source: Staff Survey (D:\Surveys\Staff\Staff.doc), questions 26, 27.

Question 1: What is our nominating process?

Nontraditional churches match people with their gifts rather than putting them on committees. In traditional churches, most nominating groups are too small. It is best if the nominating group includes one person for every twenty-five people in worship. In nontraditional churchs, nominations are not nearly as important and usually people are chosen in other ways such as through prayer and discernment. Nontraditional churches also have fewer committees.

Question 2: Do we encourage and use Spiritual Gift Inventories?

The emphasis is on how God made us, not what the institutional church needs us to do. Discovering spiritual gifts is more important than time and talent surveys that are dependent on people having some experience working in the church. Nontraditional churches are finding two ways to use the concept of gifts. One is to administer a Spiritual Gift Inventory, the other is through the guidance of a spiritual director who helps the people discern their gifts. The former is used more in boomer churches and the latter more in the buster generation. (Spiritual gifts are explained in detail in Bill Easum's book *Sacred Cows Make Gourmet Burgers,* published by Abingdon Press). You can also get our version of spiritual gifts, *Discovering Your Place in God's World,* by going to www.easumbandy.com and clicking "Store."

Action Items for Matching People with Their Skills

1. Traditional churches might want to consider finding ways to use spiritual gifts or enlarge the nominating committee so that there is one person for every twenty-five people in the average worship service.

2. Nontraditional churches might find it helpful to use both the inventory and spiritual director forms of helping people find their gifts.

Growth Principle 4: Growth Does Not Dictate That More People Will Become Inactive
(Key Questions: 2, 3-7, 9)

Data Source: Staff Survey (D:\Surveys\Staff\Staff.doc), questions 28–36.

Question 2: What are our losses?

Concentrate on the number of deaths. Is the number growing? Does it equal or surpass the number of transfers or withdrawals? Many churches find themselves getting so old that it takes more and more of the pastor's time simply to bury the members or visit them in homes. A point is reached where there is little time left to reach the unchurched after providing spiritual and physical hospice care. In the book of Acts, Stephen and others are set aside to care for the widows and orphans so that the apostles can be about the primary work of the church—reaching the unchurched. This means that although no one should be overlooked or uncared for, the hospice needs of a congregation should not be the primary responsibility of the pastor or key laypeople.

Questions 3, 4, 9: Are we assimilating?

Studies show that 80 percent of the people who drop out of the church do so within their first year. Three out of four people say they left the church because they did not feel wanted. Those who make seven or more friends within their first three months in a congregation rarely drop out. This means that people may come to the church for a variety of reasons, but they stay if they make friends. Friends are seldom made in worship. It takes a program-based church a minimum of twenty hours per month to assimilate people. For this reason, assimilation works best when a paid staff person is responsible for seeing that it is done but not necessarily being the one doing it. Recruiting volunteers is essential.

Questions 5, 6: Do we have enough small groups?

Most life-changing events occur in small groups of five to seven people. I seldom see a thriving church that does not have a major emphasis on small groups. There are various types of small groups, but the most productive are the recovery, support, learning (nurturing), and mission (ministry) groups that focus on multiplication of the group as much as anything else. Very few denominational small groups such as the women's or men's groups are reaching people born after 1950.

Question 7: How many inactive families do we have?

Inactives are seldom recoverable, so don't waste time on them. It takes ten hours to recover an inactive for every hour it takes to reach an unchurched person. It is best to concentrate on preventing inactives with outreach ministries to your members and outreach ministries to the unchurched. I recommend working with the inactives only under the following circumstances: (1) when a church has a new pastor, or (2) when the church is located in a rural area with few people. Within a new pastor's first three months, it is helpful to invite all the membership, especially the inactives, to a catered dinner to meet the pastor. See "Inactives" on our Web site. Simply go to www.easumbandy.com and click Free Resources and then FAQs.

> Hint: Most churches plateau because they do not have enough small groups that are open to new people; they reach the "single-cell ceiling." They have just enough small groups to care for the number of people presently attending. Small groups reach the saturation point and tend to become closed to new people when they: (1) have been in existence for more than six months; (2) grow beyond eight people, and the purpose of the groups' caring, sharing, and intimacy; (3) grow beyond fifteen, and the purpose is task achievement; and (4) grow beyond thirty-five and the purpose is fellowship.

Action Items for Preventing Inactives

1. Begin new groups if you do not have a small group for every fifteen people in worship. This is one of the most important issues facing your church.
2. Small churches need to recruit a volunteer to spend ten hours a week assimilating people. Larger churches need a paid staff person devoting twenty hours per month to assimilating people.

Growth Principle 5: Growth Provides a Wider Outreach to People in Need
(Key Question: 1)

> Data Source: Staff Survey (D:\Surveys\Staff\Staff.doc), question 37.

Question 1: How much money do we spend on causes outside our congregation?

The United States is now considered by the rest of the Christian world to be the third-largest mission field in the world. This means that most of a congregation's mission money needs to stay at home. A goal for effective churches is to devote 15 to 25 percent of their budget to missions. A good portion of this amount needs to be for hands-on mission in which people can participate. Usually, the more money a church gets the more it can give to missions.

Action Items for Providing a Wider Outreach

1. If the amount designated for such ministries is below 15 percent of your budget, look for ways to put more money into hands-on ministries.
2. Seek a balance between your passion for sending money away to missions and your passion for strengthening your church and growing disciples.
3. Consider developing within your church a center for church planting and staff it with a full-time paid person.

Growth Principle 6: Spiritual Leadership Is Required!
(Key Questions: 1-2, 4-13)

> Data Source: Official Body Survey Totals Spreadsheet (D:\Spreadsheets\Body Survey-Totals Spreadsheet.xls), questions 4-16.

Questions 1, 2, 4, 6, 8-10: What is the spiritual depth of
our key leaders (unpaid leaders)?

One of the most often overlooked pieces of transitioning or growing a church is the spiritual depth of the key leaders. It is essential that ministry and action flow out of hearts that are growing closer to God as the years go by. It doesn't matter how long they have been Christians. What matters is that they are growing in and exercising their faith. This can't happen without strong prayer support. Spiritual leaders never are offended by being held accountable.

Questions 5, 7, 11-13: How do our leaders serve?

It is important that service not be seen primarily as serving on committees. The most important type of service is that which is done away from the church on behalf of other people. The primary way you know your leaders are reaching some level of spiritual maturity is if they are beginning to think about and act on behalf of non-Christian people. Teams are different from committees. Teams are put together by the team leader and members are never elected to a team. In traditional churches you will regularly hear people say, "I can't wait till I finish my term and get out of this job." You will seldom hear that in nontraditional churches because people tend to serve out of gratitude rather than duty.

Action Items for Developing Spiritual Leaders

1. Cast your vision and see whose eyes light up and invite them to join you for a few months of prayer and Bible study. While doing this continue to cast your vision of what the church should become. Also, begin to talk about what spiritual accountability means. If you are a nontraditional church, you should also explore the biblical meaning of being in subjection to the authorities (usually this means the lead pastor or elders, or both).

2. Encourage your leaders to begin journaling. You will need to provide them with a template to follow.

3. If you have a heavy committee structure, begin allowing people with vision and passion to form teams to attempt some of their dreams.

Growth Principles 7 through 11: Worship, Leadership, and Ability

Growth Principle 7: Growth Will Occur When Worship Is Intentionally Emphasized (Key Questions: 1-2, 6, 10-12, 14)

Data Source: Staff Survey (D:\Surveys\Staff\Staff.doc), questions 38-46; Official Body Survey Totals Spreadsheet (D:\Spreadsheets\Body Survey-Totals Spreadsheet.xls), questions 17-22.

Questions 1-2: How important is worship?

Worship is the most important thing a human being does. Without worship, the church is nothing. Worship is a better barometer of a church's health than membership. People can join and never be discipled. People can attend without joining and still be discipled. Count your worship attendance more than your membership.

To determine if your service flows well, record your service on audiotape and get into a quiet room, shut the door, play the tape, close your eyes, and count the number of times there is no sound for more than five seconds. If there is more than one, your service does not flow well, even if the silence occurs during the prayer time.

Videotape your service and compare it with MTV programming. It might be good for your worship leaders to gather each weekend before worship to go through the mechanics of the service. The more contemporary the service, the more important it is to do this.

In traditional churches, the emphasis has been on joining the church. Nontraditional churches focus on connecting people to Jesus. Those churches that allow people to join or register a faith decision every Sunday need to leave about seven minutes for this part of the service. If your church allows people to join only at certain times, you need to make certain you are not asking them to join only when it is convenient for you. Be intentional about setting time aside each month for people to join. Look for ways to make joining the church an important step. It is all right to raise your standards for joining.

In traditional churches with more than four hundred in worship, senior pastors need to be in the pulpit on forty-four to forty-six Sundays a year. This does not mean that the senior pastor has to preach all the services. Many churches have more than one preacher on the weekend (including Sunday). In nontraditional churches, the number of times the lead pastor preaches doesn't matter.

Question 6: Do the sermons speak to our personal needs?

If the pastor's sermons are not practical enough to speak to people's personal needs, the church will have a hard time growing. It complicates matters even further if the pastor has no idea what unchurched people need. We are on a mission field today; we must meet people's basic needs first, and then we can introduce them to Christ.

Question 10: Is our worship music pleasing to a majority of the congregation?

Obviously, most people in the church are comfortable with the music or they would not be there. The key is to see if their response falls within the norm toward the positive side. If not, you should pay close attention to why they are not happy.

Question 11: What is the size of adult and youth choirs?

If a choir sings in a service, the choir needs to include one person for every ten people attending that service. Music today is just as important as the sermon. If contemporary praise teams are used, each person needs to have a microphone.

The National Endowment for the Arts asked the U.S. Census Bureau to ask the public, "What are the top three types of music you listen to?" The results were as follows: country, 51.7 percent; easy listening, 48.8 percent; rock, 43.5 percent; rhythm and blues, 40.4 percent; big band, 35.5 percent; jazz, 34.2 percent; classical, 33.6 percent; show tunes, 27.8 percent; contemporary folk, 23.1 percent; opera, 12.6 percent. There were two problems with this survey. First, the survey allowed respondents to list only three types of music. Second, the survey did not include Christian music as an option. Christian music was the fastest growing segment of the music industry in 1995.

The vast majority of growing churches today use contemporary Christian music more often than they use the hymnal and are more likely to have a band than a choir.

Question 12: What is the percentage of worship attendance
to membership?

The average percentage for all size churches is 39 percent. For churches with fewer than two hundred in worship, 60 percent. For churches with between two hundred and four hundred in worship, 45 percent. For churches with over five hundred in worship, 28 percent.

Question 14: What is our worship growth pattern?

Worship is one of the most important barometers of the church's health. There are four types of worship attendance patterns: yo-yo, declining, stable, or growing. In a church with a *yo-yo* pattern, the worship attendance goes up and down from year to year, usually peaking and bottoming out at the same basic levels. Determine if there is a yo-yo pattern. Do the tops and the bottoms of the yo-yo seem to be close to the same number every time? Yo-yo churches tend to have one of three problems. (1) They have either reached or surpassed the 80 percent of capacity limit in worship or in parking; (2) they have too many people attending for the number of paid staff; or (3) they have had pastoral changes at the point of the peak or the decline. I will discuss these problems later.

If worship attendance at your church is *declining,* it is important to ask several questions: Why are we declining? Are we content with this situation? What can we do to stop it? Are we willing to pay the price? Stopping a decline usually means new staff and new ministries.

In a church with a *stable* worship attendance pattern, the fact that the church is holding its own can be deceiving. Even though the attendance is the same as it was ten years ago, the odds are that most of the people in worship are ten years older. This means that the church is traveling along the top of a mesa, where worship attendance will eventually just fall off the edge.

If your church's worship attendance is *growing,* don't rest at ease in Zion. If it ain't broke, fix it. Are we willing to anticipate the future? How can we improve what we are doing? What new ministries do we need to begin? What programs no longer seem to be needed?

Action Items for Emphasizing Worship

1. If you are a traditional church, work out a schedule for your lead pastor to be in the pulpit forty-four to forty-six Sundays per year. If you have associate pastors who want to preach, they can do so if you have two preachers each Sunday. This will give people a choice. This is very easy to do when you have three services. However, in most traditional churches, the more an associate preaches the less likely the church will grow. This is not true in a nontraditional church.
2. Bring the membership in the choirs up to one person in the choir for every ten people in the average attendance at each service.
3. Provide a choir for each service and do not discontinue the choir's participation during the summer.
4. Set a goal to increase the ratio of the worship attendance to the membership by 10 percent over the next five years. Do not attempt to do this simply by cleaning the membership roles.
5. Decide what type of church you are and why you think you have this particular pattern.

6. Form a contemporary service that has a band and uses current music and video. Most traditional churches that do this have to have someone other than the choir director in charge of this service.
7. Perhaps the pastor needs to read some books on unchurched people, such as George Hunter's *How to Reach Secular People,* published by Abingdon Press.
8. Draw an imaginary line into the future following the downward direction of the worship attendance figures. Allow the impact of this to visually create a sense of crisis. What is going to happen to us if we do not do something?

Growth Principle 8: Growth Will Occur with the Addition of Each New Morning Service of Worship (Key Questions: 1, 3-9, 11-12, 14)

> Data Source: Staff Survey (D:\Surveys\Staff\Staff.doc), questions 47-59; Official Body Survey Totals Spreadsheet (D:\Spreadsheets\Body Survey-Totals Spreadsheet.xls), questions 23-24.

Questions 1, 8: How many worship services do we offer?

The most important decision a church can make is to add a second worship service. I know of very few traditional growing churches with one worship service. If you have just one service, look for ways to start a second, no matter how small you might be. It does not matter how empty the present worship service might be. The odds are that the present service is designed for people born before 1950. If what you have is traditional worship, make this second service very different from the present one. Usually, the addition of a worship service will increase the number of people hearing the gospel each week at your church by 12 to 20 percent in eighteen months.

Morning worship services that begin at 8:00 or 8:30 seldom reach many people, and usually when they do, most of the people are over sixty years of age. If that is your target audience, then begin the service at 8:00 or 8:30. The best time to start another service is between 9:00 and 10:00 even if you have Sunday school during that time period. There are at least ten important things to consider when starting an additional service.

1. Do not start a new service identical to what already exists. Instead, decide on one of three target audiences: busters (people born between 1965 and 1982), boomers (people born between 1946 and 1964), or seniors (people born before 1946). Each requires a different style of worship. Identify the key issues in the target audience (Do they see church as an option? When would they most likely attend? Why don't they attend now?). Focus groups with the appropriate age range can help you obtain this information.
2. Agree on the purpose for starting this new service. Make a statement of purpose that is measurable, theological, achievable, and controllable. If the service is different from what exists, refer to it as an addition, not a change. Introduce the service as an experiment that will be evaluated regularly.
3. Design the service to address the needs of the target audience. Do not plan it with the preferences of the present church members in mind.
4. Determine the time and place for the service. The fastest-growing time period in North America for worship is between 9:00 and 10:00 A.M. When you have multiple services, it is okay to have worship and Sunday school running at the same hour (it will not hurt Sunday school attendance). If you do not already have

three worship services on Sunday, put the service on Sunday morning. Weekday or Saturday services are much harder to establish than Sunday services. However, they will reach a different audience.

5. Spend at least six weeks communicating to your service area that you are starting this new service. This can be done through direct mail, announcements in the bulletin, radio, and so on. It is a mistake to start an additional service without telling the community. A good way to start such a service is to begin on the *first* Sunday in January and make a special invitation in the Christmas Eve services. Another good time to begin a new service is the second Sunday in September. In resort areas or in cold country, summer is a good time to initiate a new service.

6. Give the experiment at least a year's trial period before making any evaluations.

7. Make sure you have adequate leadership for whatever style of worship you intend to start. Multiple services are very hard on musicians, especially if they are being asked to develop an alternative style of worship. In some cases it is unfair to ask the current staff to provide a totally different service of worship. Additional part-time staff may be necessary.

8. If your target audience is busters or boomers, do not start the service until you have provided excellent child care and nursery facilities.

9. Be certain to have in place all the new support ministries you will need, such as ushers, greeters, a choir, and so on.

10. Put a follow-up procedure in place for guests.

Questions 3-6: How many worship options do we offer?

It is not uncommon today in nontraditional churches for worship to be held in more than one location with some of the services running at the same hour with either different teachers/preachers or video feeds of the message from one location to the other. Nor is it unusual for more than one preacher to be preaching each week. Satellite ministries can also help traditional churches that need space due to growth. Is there a vacant building nearby that the church can rent and use for some of its ministries?

Holding worship and Sunday school at the same hour results in more people spending only one hour at your church on Sunday; in other words, most of the newcomers will opt for worship, not Sunday school. However, most of these people would never be in Sunday school anyway and would not be in worship without an additional service. This arrangement results in more young adults attending worship and leaving their children in the nursery or Sunday school. But don't worry about a worship service during the Sunday school hour hurting Sunday school attendance. It will not; in fact, it will increase it. Some people will go to worship instead of going home while their children are in Sunday school. In time, some will commit to two hours.

Question 7: When was the newest service started?

In traditional churches it is usually effective to allow a new service to have eighteen months to develop before starting another service. Nontraditional churches don't seem to follow any rules here.

Question 9: Does each service have a regular choir or band?

In a traditional church it is essential to have a separate choir for every worship service. Do not rotate the choirs or allow a service to exist without its own choir.

Rotation between services is hard on old habits. It is good to allow adults to sing at two services if they wish. In a nontraditional church it does not matter if there is a choir. It is essential that if there is a group or ensemble that leads worship each member has a microphone. In a nontraditional church it is normal for every service to have a band.

Questions 11-12: On how many Sundays each year does our adult choir sing?

Healthy churches that have choirs do not cancel their regular choirs in the summer. When relocating, most persons move near the end of the school year, and after getting settled they start looking for a church in July and August or on Christmas Eve night. The number one time unchurched young families and singles go to church is Christmas Eve. Easter is not nearly as fertile a field for reaching the unchurched as Christmas Eve. In anticipation of holiday travel, many churches have shut down their systems after the choral presentation the Sunday prior to Christmas Eve. In a similar manner, a signal is given to people when the church cuts back on their programs during the summer. When churches reduce their schedules during the summer, they tell people that it is okay to take a vacation from the organized body of Christ. This translates to many that faith is not really the most essential part of our life. Unless the church presents faith (experienced in the worship of God) as the most important aspect of our lives, persons born after 1950 do not take the church seriously. Continue worship at the same hours during the summer. Continue Sunday school during the summer. Continue the choir during the summer. The adult choir should sing even when the children's choirs sing. If you live in a warm climate, air-condition at least the sanctuary.

In nontraditional churches it is normal for the band to play year round. The service isn't a service without the music.

Question 14: How many Christmas Eve services does our church offer?

As I have already noted, Christmas Eve is one of the most important days of the year. Often, more first-time visitors will attend on this night than on any other day of the year. Send out a Christmas card to every home within a thirty-minute drive from the church inviting them to the Christmas Eve services. The most popular times for worship on Christmas Eve night are 5:00, 7:00, 9:00, and 11:00. Candlelight is advised. Families with children might be encouraged to attend at 4:30 or 5:00 (let the children present a musical); a contemporary service may be offered at 7:00; a candlelight service with communion may be held at 9:00; and a traditional service may be offered at 11:00. However, in most areas attendance at the 11:00 service is waning.

Action Items for Adding Worship Services

1. If you have only one service, add one that is different from the present one. Focus on the largest adult age group in the area within ten miles of the church.
2. If your largest service on Sunday morning is 80 percent full, start another service on Sunday morning no matter how many services you already have on Sunday morning.
3. If you are a traditional church and do not have a regular choir in an existing service, develop one for that service.
4. If your choir does not sing every Sunday in each service, ask it to do so.

5. If any of your present Christmas Eve services are 80 percent full, add another Christmas Eve service.
6. If you are a traditional church with a contemporary service, make sure there is a contemporary service on Easter and Christmas.
7. Nontraditional churches should experiment with multiple preachers.

Growth Principle 9: Growth Is Directly Related to the Leadership Strength of the Pastor (Key Questions: 3-4, 6-16)

> Data Source: Staff Survey (D:\Surveys\Staff\Staff.doc), questions 60-62; Official Body Survey Totals Spreadsheet (D:\Spreadsheets\Body Survey-Totals Spreadsheet.xls), questions 25-37.

Questions 3-4: Do we experience long pastorates?

The average pastoral tenure in growing churches in the twenty-first century is fifteen to twenty years. The same is true for staff. When there is a match between the pastor or staff members and the church, encourage the pastor and staff to stay. However, the longer the pastor and staff stay, the more time away they will need for reflection and personal growth. Churches that change pastors every two or three years usually have some deep-seated problem within the lay leadership or they are very small churches that just can't keep a pastor because of limited finances.

Questions 6-16: Is our pastor a leader?

For the relevant data, see questions 27-37 on the Official Body Survey Totals Spreadsheet (D:\Spreadsheets\Body Survey-Totals Spreadsheet.xls). The average score among two hundred churches surveyed for questions 6-16 is 2.30. If you compare the average of these scores with the scores on Growth Principle 1, question 7, and Growth Principle 7, question 6, they should be within .50 in either direction to be reliable.

I have never seen a church whose transforming vision began with someone other than the pastor. I am sure it happens, but I think it is rare. In growing churches the pastor and staff must take the laity where they would not go on their own. Mistakes are inevitable when churches are traveling into new areas. Pastors must delegate everything possible. The more they delegate, the more laity blossom and the more people are reached for Christ.

Some pastors are very effective in a church of one size and not effective in a church of another size. This is because churches of different sizes need different types of leadership skills (see the chart below). The world into which we are moving will be a diverse world of choices. To reach this world, pastors will have to be able to converse with a wide variety of lifestyles and value systems without feeling threatened. The ability to mediate between generations is essential. If the composite score of these answers is .50 above the average, ask why.

Relationship between Stages of a Growing Church and Leadership Skills Needed				
Stage of Development	Tendency in Attitude	Church Process Needs	Reason	Leadership Skills
0-199*	Survival "Water testers" "We can't do that"	Recruitment	Ministry needs larger than pool	Catalyst, Change agent, Risk taker, Partnership, Entrepreneurial
200-499*	Resistance to change "We have arrived"	Training	Difficulty assimilating change; Pastoral staff overworked and ministry understaffed	Anticipates, adjusts to, and interprets change; Chief Operating Officer; Prioritize
500-999*	Confused about role of staff, laity, policy and procedure	Identifying	Large size and unknown quantity of pool	Visionary Decision maker Delegation
1000+*	Aloof Cold Fragile Tradition	Deploying	Reliance on staff and not enough staff	Preacher and Strategist

*Denotes average worship size

Action Items for Valuing the Leadership Strength of the
Pastor

1. If there is a match between your pastor and the church and if your pastor has the talent or is willing to develop the skills to lead the church, what do you need to do to keep the pastor for fifteen to twenty years?
2. Provide a minimum of fifteen hundred dollars in your budget per program staff person for continuing education.
3. If you are a traditional church, provide one program staff person for every one hundred people in worship, including children.
4. If the pastoral scores are way out of the norm to the negative side, encourage your pastor to work on his or her skills; however, make sure that a handful of people did not drive up the average by marking eight, nine, or ten on all the scores.

Growth Principle 10: Growth Is Directly Related to the Attitude of the Paid Staff (Key Questions: 1, 2, 6-7, 9-11, 18, 19)

Data Source: Official Body Survey Totals Spreadsheet (D:\Spreadsheets\Body Survey-Totals Spreadsheet.xls), questions 38-42; Staff Survey (D:\Surveys\Staff\ Staff.doc), questions 63-76.

Question 1: What is the main responsibility of the paid
staff?

Healthy churches do not pay staff to do ministry. Staff is paid to equip the laity to do ministry. Staff does not replace volunteers. Staff identifies laity for ministry, recruits and deploys laity into ministry, and equips laity for ministry. The key text here is Ephesians 4:11-12. Hiring staff to do ministry is the number one mistake of traditional churches.

Most staff should be able to begin paying for themselves in two years through the number of volunteers they bring into the church. If you have the right staff you will begin to see the number of volunteers/servants grow exponentially.

Question 2: How many paid staff do we have?

The goal in a traditional church is to have the equivalent of one full-time paid program person for every hundred people in worship (including children, even if they are not in worship). More staff is needed today than in the 1950s because the world we live in today is far more complicated. In the 1950s, the nuclear family of Mom, Dad, and the kids came to church. Today, there are many types of families. In the 1950s, the church had very little competition for the lives of children and youth. Today, the church finds itself competing with a variety of things that pull children and youth away from the church. In the 1950s, the Judeo-Christian value system was reinforced in the home, the schools, and the church. Today, only the church reinforces the Judeo-Christian value system. Drugs and gangs were not nearly as widespread in the 1950s as they are today. Today, people are more mobile than they were in the 1950s and most often do not have an extended family nearby to help in times of crisis. In other words, it is far more difficult today than it was in the 1950s to minister to people and to equip them for a life that follows Jesus Christ.

Program staff includes the pastor and any paid staff members who work directly with people, with the exception of part-time musicians who are support staff. Music directors are considered program people only if they are serving as the equivalent of a full-time staff person and are constantly increasing the number of people involved in the church's music programs. Program staff should be able to function, most of the time, on their own with minimal input from the senior pastor.

The primary role of the lead pastor is to create an environment in which people are transformed and grow in Christ rather than being a nuts-and-bolts type of pastor. The larger the church, the truer this is. Support staff includes the organist, the pianist, any children's choir leaders, all handbell players, secretaries, custodians, administrators, business managers, and so on.

If the area around your church is highly populated, it is not necessary to be able to afford the staff when you hire them. If you have enough money to pay them for one year, and you get the right staff, they should be paying their way in one and a half years.

Count your present program and support staff in terms of total full-time staff members. (For example, two half-time staff members equal one full-time staff member.)

The best order in which to bring program staff on board is (1) Worship Leader; (2) Lay Mobilizer; and (3) Outreach (evangelism). Do not make the mistake of most churches and make your first hire a youth director. Start with worship and succeeding hiring will be more affordable.

Nontraditional churches will find that it is almost always better to hire from within the church than to go looking elsewhere. They also find that academic credentials aren't nearly as important as demonstrated credentials so they focus on skill and passion rather than credentials.

Questions 6-7: How do the pastor and the staff relate?

If the scores from questions 39-40 on the Official Body Survey are over 3.10, investigate the relationship between the pastor and the staff.

Questions 9-11, 18, 19: How are staff meetings managed?

These questions are important only if you have the equivalent of more than two full-time people on staff. The primary role of the senior pastor in multiple staff settings is to cast vision. See chapter 7 of Bill Easum's book *Sacred Cows Make Gourmet Burgers*. Staff meetings need to be held weekly or daily for short periods of time. Staff meetings should be more vision oriented than nuts and bolts. Don't do "calendaring" at staff meetings. Have someone do it before and hand it out at the staff meeting.

The larger the staff, the more important retreats become. Poor time management is rampant in church staffs. Most cities have short-term business courses on time management. If these are too expensive, see if you have a member who either teaches time management or knows someone who could volunteer to come in and work with the staff.

Action Items for Encouraging a Growth-Oriented Attitude among the Paid Staff

1. Pay staff only to *equip* laity to do ministry and then get out of the way. If you are paying staff to *do* ministry, you may need to compose new job descriptions.
2. If you are a traditional church, add enough staff to equal one staff person for every one hundred people in worship. If you are a nontraditional church, hire enough staff to equal one full-time person for every one hundred in worship up to two hundred, and then one for every two hundred thereafter.
3. Before hiring, have a clear picture of where your church is going and how this new staff will help you get there.
4. Don't be afraid to hire from within.

Growth Principle 11: Growth Is Directly Related to the Unpaid Staff's Perception of the Congregation's Size and Ability Rather than Reality (Key Questions: 1-19)

Data Source: Staff Survey (D:\Surveys\Staff\Staff.doc), questions 77-80; Official Body Survey Totals Spreadsheet (D:\Spreadsheets\Body Survey-Totals Spreadsheet.xls), questions 43-57.

Question 1: Are we small, medium, or large?

Most churches do not realize how large they really are compared to other churches. The more clearly they understand their comparable size, the easier it is for them to take bigger steps of faith.

Questions 2-3: What is our perception of our size?

These two questions give you a reality check on how the leadership perceives the size of the church. Comparing the answer to question 2 with the answer to question 1 will show you how accurate or inaccurate your leadership's perception is.

Questions 4-15: How is our lay leadership functioning?

The composite average of all the scores for questions 4-15 is 4.1. You will notice this is higher (more negative) than the average of the scores evaluating the pastor's leadership. (I've never seen a church where the scores for the laity were lower than those for the pastor; if your church is an exception, please call me!) This means that laity do not appreciate their own skills as much as they do their pastor's. If you want your church to grow, the laity need to understand that they have incredible spiritual gifts to offer to the body of Christ. Raising the leadership's understanding of their importance to actual ministry is essential. As churches grow, leadership requires a considerable amount of training in order to keep up with the accompanying dynamics of growth. Leaders in small churches operate differently than leaders in a large church. For example, personnel committees can evaluate a pastor, but it is impossible for them to evaluate three or four staff people they never observe on the job. As the church grows, it is best if the pastor evaluates the rest of the staff or if the staff evaluates one another. Trustee committees can handle property issues in a small, Sunday-only church. In a larger, seven-day-a-week church, it is impossible for trustees to care for the property in a timely fashion.

All finance and trustee people will benefit from a good, solid training session on the best way to be good stewards of the foundation money in light of the different ways in which baby boomers and busters approach the subject of money. An excellent book on this subject is Lyle Schaller's *44 Ways to Increase the Financial Base of Your Church.* In churches with over two hundred in worship, personnel and finance people will benefit from reading Lyle Schaller's *The Larger Church and the Multiple Staff. The Abingdon Guide to Funding Ministry* is an outstanding almanac for good stewards. *Giving and Stewardship in an Effective Church,* by Kennon Callahan, is also excellent. (See Recommended Reading on our Web site. Simply go to www.easumbandy.com, click Free Resources, then click Library.)

Question 16: How long do lay leaders lead?

In traditional churches, it tends to be best to limit the tenure of people holding office to three years to avoid power blocs within the decision-making process and to avoid burnout among people who are not power hungry. Also, such problems are less likely to occur among those people who are truly exercising their spiritual gifts. Nontraditional churches can ignore this question.

Question 19: How do we raise up leaders?

Adult leadership is *the* most important component to a thriving church. It is essential to have some form of farm system for raising up future leaders. This system needs to be one that takes people from being non-Christian to being the spiritual leadership of your church.

Action Items for Improving Perception of Ability

1. Provide training sessions for lay leaders to learn the differences between how a small church and a large church function.
2. If your composite average for the scores to questions 4-15 on the Ministry Audit falls above 4.45, you need to work on leadership development or self-image or conflict management.
3. Have your church members read Lyle Schaller's *The Larger Church and the Multiple Staff,* published by Abingdon Press.

4. I recommend that all lay leaders read the following books: *Unfreezing Moves* and *Sacred Cows Make Gourmet Burgers* by Bill Easum, and George S. Hunter III's *How to Reach Secular People* and *Church for the Unchurched,* published by Abingdon Press.

5. If you do not have a system for raising up new leaders, design one and implement it.

Growth Principles 12 through 16: Space, Distance, and Visitors

Growth Principle 12: When 80 Percent of Any Space Is in Use, It Is Time to Start Making Plans for More Space (Key Questions: 1, 3-4, 6-11)

Data Source: Staff Survey (D:\Surveys\Staff\Staff.doc), questions 81-92; Official Body Survey Totals Spreadsheet (D:\Spreadsheets\Body Survey-Totals Spreadsheet.xls), questions 58-59.

Question 1: What level of commitment do we expect?

A high level of commitment is one of the key factors I see in every growing congregation. God does not honor leadership that is half-committed. If the majority of your leadership does not answer "high," you need to raise your church's expectations concerning its commitment level. This begins with a deeper appreciation of what it means to be a servant of Jesus Christ and of the absolute uniqueness of what the Christian church has to offer. Among the staff and key lay leaders is where this deeper commitment must begin. Usually, the problem lies with staff and laity who feel entitled to grace and do not act as role models of commitment.

Question 3: How much space can we use?

Anytime any facility is 80 percent full, it is time to provide more space. It is next to impossible to sustain growth beyond the comfort level of 80 percent capacity. This applies to everything the church does. The 80 percent rule is an invisible but powerful presence that works like the law of gravity. No one will tell you he or she is not coming back because the sanctuary, nursery, parking lot, or Sunday school class is more than 80 percent full. In fact, no one really notices that the space is 80 percent full. It just feels uncomfortable. In the western states, the comfort level can be as low as 75 percent.

Question 4: Do we need more worship space?

Anytime your main worship service is 80 percent full, growth is seldom sustained over a two-year period without adding another service or more space. If you do not do this, nothing else will matter. Consider this: It is immoral to continue to allow people to join the church while your worship attendance average remains the same because the primary worship service is too full. The same is true for parking. Educate your leadership on this important item. If your worship attendance average has been up and down like a yo-yo over a ten-year period, one of three things will be true: (1) you have had a new pastor at each high attendance point; (2) your largest worship service is at the 80 percent limit; or (3) your parking is at the 80 percent limit.

Question 6: Do we need more space for the choirs?

A full choir is good, but it does discourage people from joining the choir. Perhaps you need more choirs or you need to start that second or third service so that each service has its own choir.

Question 7: Do we need more nursery space?

The nursery needs to be the nicest room in the church. It also needs to be on the same level as the sanctuary. A paid sitter who also recruits volunteers is essential. It is also best if there is some consistency in the attendance of this person. Parents are used to seeing a familiar face when they drop their children off at day care.

The nursery should be open anytime the church is open. Separate the cribbers, crawlers, and walkers. Provide the visitors with a small brochure on the nursery. In growing churches it is best to require identification from parents as they are leaving a child in the nursery. Some churches require parents or caretakers to leave their drivers' licenses. Remember that kidnapping by noncustodial parents is a major problem. Check under "Nursery" on our Web site. Simply go to www.easumbandy.com and click Free Resources and then FAQs.

Question 8: Do we need more education space?

This question is important only for traditional churches. Small groups that meet in homes take the place of supplement Sunday school in nontraditional churches.

Questions 9-11: Are the Sunday school classes full?

If any classes are filled to over 80 percent capacity, rearrange the classes to avoid as much of the problem as possible. Often, churches have small groups of older people meeting in rooms much too large and large groups of younger people meeting in rooms much too small because the older groups have met where they are for a long time (they used to need the space). Classes that do not want to move to make room for more people to learn about God do not understand what it means to follow Christ. If there are no rooms available, consider having classes in the pastor's office, in the kitchen, in hallways, and wherever you can find space.

Action Items for Providing Adequate Space

1. If the commitment level is not high, step up the preaching and teaching on servanthood. Staff should be role models of higher commitment. I am not suggesting that the solution is simply that "staff should try harder"; rather, I am emphasizing how the staff's commitment affects a congregation's perceptions of its own ability.
2. If you are over the 80 percent mark in worship, the first step is to add another service or a larger sanctuary or both.
3. If your choirs are full, provide more choir space or assign one distinct choir to each worship service.
4. Make the necessary nursery changes indicated by your analysis under question 7. This is one of the most important and urgent changes to make.
5. If your Sunday school is too full, either add another service, build, or start a small-group ministry that meets in homes. For small-group material, see the resources listed under "Small Group Ministries" on our Web site. Simply go to www.easumbandy.com and click Free Resources and then FAQs.
6. Find another location for Sunday school classes that are filled to over 80 percent of capacity.

Growth Principle 13: Growth Is Encouraged When Parking Is Adequate
(Key Questions: 1-8)

Data Source: Staff Survey (D:\Surveys\Staff\Staff.doc), questions 93-99; Official Body Survey Totals Spreadsheet (D:\Spreadsheets\Body Survey-Totals Spreadsheet.xls), question 60.

Question 1: Does our church own enough land?

A minimum amount of land for a church in the twenty-first century is ten acres. Most churches planning on effective ministry are purchasing over thirty acres. If you plan to persist as a regional church, you must have eight acres. If you plan on being a megachurch (ten thousand or more in worship) you need at least sixty acres.

Questions 2-8: How many parking spaces do we need?

To figure out how many parking spaces you need, simply follow the directions. On question 2 make sure that you count the average attendance of the largest worship service during the previous year. The national average used in planning parking for major malls is 1.75 people per car. As we move further into the twenty-first century, more people will come to church in a ratio of one person per car. Studies also show that people tend not to walk more than six hundred feet to a door. Church parking lots are much like those at malls. If you plan on building a parking garage, keep in mind that people tend not to use them if it takes more than eight minutes to leave the garage.

When building a new sanctuary or developing a master plan, do not place the sanctuary near the street in front of the parking. Instead, put the parking lot in front of and around the sanctuary or other buildings. Many churches make the mistake of relying on using the parking lot of a nearby business, such as a bank or a supermarket. I know of one church that had virtually no off-street parking of its own, but they had all the parking they needed across the street at a large Sears store. They never dreamed the store would go out of business, but it did, and the church's attendance is rapidly declining.

You can determine the worth of each new parking space by dividing the number of present spaces into the total amount of money you received last year. Every time you reach 80 percent of your capacity, find a way to add 20 percent more parking. There are many ways to do this: (1) The staff and members of the official body who have no trouble walking can covenant together to park on the street in order to leave room for the "yet-to-be-committed"; and (2) You may want to use the "one, two, three" method of parking used by a growing number of churches. People park bumper to bumper in rows for one-hour parking, two-hour parking, and three-hour parking. Attendants in the lot help people find the right row. One car is always kept on hand for anyone to use in case of an emergency. Provide a parking lot just for visitors.

Action Items for Providing Adequate Parking

1. Add enough parking to provide one space for every two people on the property at the peak hour.
2. Alternately, start a "one, two, three" method of parking in rows.
3. Alternately, obtain a lease on adjacent property and use that property for parking.
4. Alternately, bus your leadership from nearby parking lots.

5. Encourage the staff, members of the official body, and choir members who are in good health to sign a covenant to park off the property. Leaders today need to be seen as servants. The staff should lead the way.

Growth Principle 14: Growth Can Occur Even Though the Church Cannot Afford to Build (Key Questions: 3-6)

Data Source: Staff Survey (D:\Surveys\Staff\Staff.doc), questions 100-105.

Questions 3-5: What is our total and potential debt?

Two rules of thumb for debt are helpful: (1) Keep the amount of debt service (monthly mortgage) under 28 percent of the operating budget; and (2) keep the total amount of money owed at or under two times the present operating budget, including the debt service. If you are a rapidly growing church, it is possible to build even when all you have in the bank is eighteen months of debt service payments. You can engage in a bond program. There are three ways to administer bond programs: (1) sell all the bonds, mostly to members of your church; (2) hire someone to sell the bonds, in and out of your church; and (3) contract with a bond company to loan you the money and sell the bonds to their clients. More and more churches are paying for new construction as they go so that they do not owe anything after they move in.

Question 6: When was our last building program?

Fast-growing churches can build every two or three years because of the number of new people who are joining. Unfortunately, some people believe that if they build a facility, people will show up. This has not proved to be true, especially for educational facilities. Something significant has to be happening inside the new facility that addresses a felt need of the community. In the case of a new sanctuary, if the church is providing significant ministries and the area is growing, there is usually a 25 to 30 percent jump in worship attendance the day the new sanctuary is opened. Before you build, read *When Not To Build* by Ray Bowman and Eddy Hall, published by Baker Books.

Action Items for Deciding Whether You Can Build
1. How you fund the project does not matter if the mortgage payment, including debt service, is below 28 percent of your total budget.
2. See appendix 4: Evaluating the Site, Property, and Facilities.

Growth Principle 15: Growth Can Occur without Merely Transferring Members from One Church to Another (Key Question:s 1, 4-6, 8, 9, 10, 11, 12)

Data Source: Staff Survey (D:\Surveys\Staff\Staff.doc), questions 106-117; The Worship Survey Totals Spreadsheet (D:\Spreadsheets\Worship Survey-Totals Spreadsheet.xls); Chamber of Commerce.

Question 1: How are people joining our church?

How people are joining is very important, even though membership loss or growth means very little to the health of a church. Most mainline churches will lose 50 percent of their present membership to death over the next twenty-five years. It is better for churches to focus on worship attendance than on membership. The goal is for the people joining by profession of faith (unchurched people) to outnumber the total of people joining by any other method. It is not healthy if the majority of the professions of faith are by confirmation of youth. So the number in the second column is very important. The farther we go into the twenty-first century, the more likely people will have no church background.

Questions 4-6: How far do our members drive?

The number of miles and minutes people drive to work often determines the number of miles and minutes people will drive to church, especially if the church is located along the same route they drive to work.

Question 8: Who are the unchurched in our area?

If you do not have a demographic study, call the Chamber of Commerce to get this information. Churches make a major mistake when they ask their members what should be done to reach the community. Church members have very little understanding of the needs of people who have never gone to church. Once a person has been a member of a church for five years, they have a difficult time understanding the needs of the unchurched.

Question 9: Which group is not being adequately ministered to?

Often it makes no sense to do something that other churches just like you are doing. Ask yourself whether these churches are just like you and whether what they are doing is of significant quality. Are they targeting the same kind of people you are? Look for the gaps, where your church can do what other churches are not doing and reach people whom other churches are not reaching.

Questions 10, 11: Is the population of our county or region growing, and are we keeping pace?

If the population of the area has grown over the past ten years, the church should have grown at or beyond the same rate. However, just because the population is not growing does not mean that the church should not grow. Studies show that communities that experience "turnover" are just as fertile to the church as areas that experience population growth. Turnover growth happens when younger families move into a community as older members of the community move away.

Question 12: Are the schools in our area full?

If the schools are full, the church should be full of children. However, often the schools are full of children of different ethnicities than those within the church. This raises a question of morality for the local congregation. Is the church ignoring a minority in the area or has the area changed so much that the majority is now the minority? If that is the case, what do you need to do to reach the changing neighborhood?

Action Items for Seeking Nontransfer Growth

1. Obtain a demographic study or call the Chamber of Commerce to learn more about the community.

2. Decide if the answer to question 9 is worth pursuing.
3. Strategize about how you can reach more adults by profession of faith.
4. What ways can you better become acquainted with your neighborhood?

Growth Principle 16: Growth Almost Always Occurs if the Congregation Is Friendly toward Visitors (Key Questions: 1-3, 5-6, 8, 9-10, 14, 17, 19)

> Data Source: Staff Survey (D:\Surveys\Staff\Staff.doc), questions 118-132; Official Body Survey Totals Spreadsheet (D:\Spreadsheets\Body Survey-Totals Spreadsheet.xls), questions 61-65.

Question 1: How much advertising do we do?

The larger the church, the more important it is to spend 5 percent of the budget for advertising. The Yellow Pages are the place to begin. Place an ad that stands out and gives a clue about the nature of the church. Avoid the newspaper unless you put your ad in the entertainment or sports sections. Radio advertising during drive time is an excellent way for churches of all sizes to target the people they are trying to reach. Direct mail is useful if you mail to the same people six times during the year. The only exception to this rule is a Christmas card inviting people in the community to the Christmas Eve services. Television is very helpful to large churches with over a thousand in worship. Thirty-second television spots six or more times during the week, supplemented by a broadcast of either the worship service or a portion of the worship service on Sunday and at one other time during the week are good. Flyers are the most useless form of advertising. Churches small and large are placing home pages on the World Wide Web. These advertisements include e-mail boxes for the staff, announcements, service times, and links to sites all over the Internet. The cost of advertising in cyberspace is less expensive but that might change in the next few years.

Questions 2, 3: How many new families visit each week
and how many join?

These are important indicators of the future growth of a church. The goal is to contact all the people who visit your church (including the people from out of town you may never see again). Studies show that traditional churches must respond within twenty-four hours to those who decide to give you their names, addresses, and phone numbers. This contact needs to be personal and made by the pastor in a church with fewer than four hundred in worship and by laypeople in the larger church. The layperson can call the visitor on the phone or make what some call a "doorstep visit," taking a gift of some kind and not going inside the door. The key to assimilating new people is introducing them to five to seven new people whom they will consider to be good friends within the first three months of their visiting.

Questions 5, 6: Are we contacting unchurched people?

Studies show that growing churches spend a minimum of twenty hours per week seeking ways to reach and respond to those unchurched people around them and those who attend. The staff does research and training, and laypeople do the research and responding. In small churches, usually the pastor responds to visitors. Often, in order to allow the pastor to do this, churches have to reduce the number of meetings they require the pastor to attend. As the church grows, laypeople are trained to do most of the responding to visitors. In nontraditional churches, the major emphasis is on getting new people into small groups.

Question 8: Is every church event a point of entry?

Use every event as an opportunity to invite people to consider the Christian faith and as an opportunity to register the people attending. This applies to everything: musicals, bazaars, fairs, community dinners (consider offering a door prize at the appropriate events so that you can get names, addresses, and phone numbers from the registration forms). Be sure to follow up within the week on those who sign in. Churches tend to make the mistake of not seeing all events as an opportunity to reach into the lives of the unchurched. The best example is weekday childcare. Many churches rent out their facilities to childcare services instead of offering these services themselves. This is a major mistake. Weekday childcare has been one of the best ways to reach into the lives of the unchurched. A church should avoid focusing solely on its membership.

Questions 9, 10: Are we building a mailing list?

Put visitors on the mailing list the first time they register. Send them a letter from the pastor, the newsletter, and a gift and invite them to a small group. The invitation should be extended by the small-group leader or by a friend within the small group.

Studies show that friendly, brief visits to first-time visitors within thirty-six hours after they attend will cause 85 percent of them to return the following week. If this home visit is made within seventy-two hours, 60 percent will return. If it is made more than seven days later, 15 percent will return. If the pastor makes this call, each result is cut in half. A phone call by a layperson or the pastor instead of a personal visit cuts results by 80 percent. This immediate response by a layperson is the most important factor in reaching first-time visitors. The average person today visits several churches before deciding on a church. This means he or she may not come back for six weeks. By then, the average person decides which church to return to based on the friendliness and helpfulness of the members. If you wait until they return the second time, you lose 85 percent of your visitors.

Concentrate on building your prospect list. You can pick up names from Sunday registration, from contacts members encounter in the daily routine of business, from real estate transfers, from marriage notices in local newspapers, from families who move into homes next-door to members, from the welcome wagon, from birth notices, and from registration forms for any church programs attended by visitors.

Think of newcomers as "guests" instead of "visitors," and members as "hosts" instead of "greeters." Develop a consistent and workable registration of your visitors at every service, including the Christmas Eve service. The typical registration pad is not the best way to take registration. It does not get most people to register, nor does it get any confidential information. By the time the pad gets to the end of the pew, the rest of the worshippers are doing something else and there is no pressure to sign in. If the pad is passed back to the original position, everyone has the opportunity to see who is on the roll. This is not good because many unchurched boomers and busters want to be anonymous.

Instead of the traditional registration pad, place individual, confidential response cards in the bulletins or on the backs of the pews. Everyone registers at the same time. Encourage everyone to write any prayer requests on the back of the cards and fold them over. Take registration during worship and have the ushers collect the cards right then. Do not do it before the worship service begins. Allow guests in worship to be anonymous if they wish. Do not single them out during worship by asking them to hold up their hands or having them stand or having the members stand. Do not pass the traditional registration pad down the aisle and ask the people to see who on the row is a guest and say hello to them.

Question 14: Do we designate visitor parking?

Designate ten parking spaces for visitors close to the sanctuary door. Paint "Guests" on the curb, car stops, or pavement, and put signs up telling visitors that such parking exists. Downtown churches with limited parking need to change "reserved for staff" to "reserved for visitors" on Sunday. Downtown churches with on-street parking can put out A-shaped signs that say "Visitor Parking" and take them down after worship.

Question 17: Do we provide information packets for visitors?

No one should leave a church without having the opportunity to take information home or receive it in the mail. The younger the person, the more important it is that the information be available on a short video instead of print.

Question 19: Do we have a decision booth?

Information booths for people arriving is one thing; it is quite another thing to have a decision booth after worship where people can share any spiritual decision they made during worship. In the case of salvation, they can receive prayer and a packet full of resources for new Christians. To see a decision booth called "Say Yes" go to http://easumbandy.com/resources/index.php?action=details&record=1154.

Action Items to Capture Visitors

1. Provide 5 percent of your budget for advertising.
2. Set a goal of doubling the number of first-time visitors if you have fewer than five per week.
3. Respond to visitors within twenty-four hours. Use laypeople.
4. Establish a gift ministry. This means having laypeople deliver a plant, a loaf of bread, or some gift made or grown by the congregation to first-time families within two hours of their visit. To do this you will need color-coded registration cards—one color for members and one for visitors. Take up the cards during worship, sort them during worship, and have the gift, a map, and the gift card ready to be picked up by volunteers after worship and delivered on their way home. Most cities have vendors that provide 8" x 11" "key" maps that break the city into small segments. These are the best kind of maps to give to the people delivering the gifts. Request that the volunteers not go inside; these are "doorstep visits." Using this method, people do not have to go home and then go back out. They can deliver the gift on the way home. Be sure to register attendance on Christmas Eve night.
5. The staff needs to spend twenty hours a week on evangelism.
6. Look at the events you have planned and find ways to involve unchurched people in them.
7. Build up the visitors' mailing list by putting first-time visitors on the list.
8. Provide more visitor parking.

9. If you have access to the World Wide Web, use your Web browser to search for the word *worship* and check out how many churches are advertising or conducting communications through the Internet. This number will continue to grow as a major source of communicating with the baby busters and millennials over the coming years.

Growth Principles 17 through 19: Money, Planning, and Change

Growth Principle 17: Asking for Money Encourages Growth (Key Questions: 1, 4-6, 9-11, 14, 17, 19-21, 26, 28)

> Data Source: Staff Survey (D:\Surveys\Staff\Staff.doc), questions 133-158; Official Body Survey Totals Spreadsheet (D:\Spreadsheets\Body Survey-Totals Spreadsheet.xls), questions 66-68.

Question 1: What are our budget totals?

For the purpose of this section, combine operating and building budgets into one figure. The vast majority of churches have seen their budgets increase over the past ten years even though their worship attendance is declining. Increasing income is never a sign of strength or vitality. However, since that fateful day of September 11, 2001, many church and denominational budgets have begun to decline. We expect this trend to become much worse in traditional churches over the next two decades.

Question 4: Do we do a pledge drive for the annual budget?

Traditional churches need to do annual pledge drives for the budget and involve at least one-fourth of their congregations in the preparation for the actual week or Sunday of gathering the pledges. A minimum of three weeks' preparation is necessary so that everyone is aware of the coming pledge drive and has time to think about his or her pledge. Traditional churches that do not do a pledge drive are losing a sizable portion of their potential income. Traditional churches need to hold a stewardship drive each year if they want to develop solid stewards and budgets. Most churches that rely on a "faith promise" type of stewardship seldom have an annual average giving of one thousand dollars per person in worship, including children.

Nontraditional churches may be more likely to focus exclusively on tithing and beyond tithing for their income. They may not do capital fund drives for large projects or they may raise the money up-front. In these churches, tithing is expected of all of its key leaders and is considered to be a goal for everyone in the church. Traditional churches transitioning to nontraditional need to exercise great caution in making the shift from pledging to tithing. In most cases it takes years to make this transition.

Nontraditional churches that do not do pledge drives can skip questions 4-11, 14-18.

Questions 5, 6: When and how often is our pledge drive?

The best time to conduct a stewardship drive is usually between January and Mother's Day. This means that pledges would not follow a calendar year.

Questions 9-11: What is our average pledge?

Is the actual number of pledges increasing? Is the average amount of the pledges increasing each year? Growing churches need only 70 percent of their budget covered by the pledges. As the church grows beyond a half-million-dollar budget, the percentage of the budget covered by pledges needs to decrease.

If you have demographics for the area, you need to consider the relation between your budget and the average household income of your members. The goal is for the average family to give 3.5 to 5 percent of its total household income to the church. Average church members in traditional churches give around 2.5 percent of their annual household income. In an exceptional church the average giving will reach up to 5 percent of the annual household income. Also, the more money people make and the larger the home they live in, the smaller the percentage of their income they tend to give.

Question 14: Do we contact new members for a pledge?

Traditional churches need to be intentional about asking new members for pledges within the first month after they join. Develop a method of getting a pledge from each new member of the church. Perhaps start asking them during the membership class. You may want to develop a team of laity who feel comfortable calling those who have not made a pledge. As soon as a person joins, the pastor should send him or her a letter of welcome. This letter should be followed by a letter from the finance chairperson explaining the mission and ministry of the church and its cost. This letter should focus on the mission and ministry, not the financial cost. Enclose a commitment card. If the new members do not return the card within two weeks, do no more at this time until they are welcomed into a small group. Many nontraditional churches (much like synagogues) require a pledge before joining, though many nontraditional independent churches prefer not to have "membership."

Question 17: How are our stewardship campaigns
conducted?

It is best not to use the same stewardship campaign more than two or three years in a row. Churches with over three hundred in worship with a large number of people born between 1946 and 1964 need to consider "target stewardship" instead of generic mailings. Targeted stewardship is customizing mailings and small-group sessions around the actual amount people are presently giving to the church. To see such a program go to www.easumbandy.com and click "Store."

Question 19: Do we encourage designated giving?

Designated giving always results in more income in traditional churches and better stewards if a large portion of the congregation is under forty-five years of age. Designated giving will not harm the general budget of a traditional church. Non-traditional churches talk about second-mile giving or "beyond the tithe" giving.

Question 20: Do we have regular special offerings?

It will help traditional churches to have two or three special offerings for the budget during the year: at Easter, during summer, and at Christmas.

Question 21: How much does each worshipper give?

The minimum goal for a traditional church is to reach an average annual gift of one thousand to fifteen hundred dollars per person, including children. The amount is double in nontraditional churches.

Question 26: What are our financial resources?

Many traditional churches have enough money squirreled away in a variety of accounts to turn themselves around. Often these funds have been lying around in these accounts for several years. No one is ever helped to mature in Christ by money gaining interest in the bank. Your task is to put that money to good use. Quit waiting for a rainy day. How much of this money absolutely cannot be used? How much is really designated for a specific item or ministry? It is better to use this money for new ministries or staff that you are certain will meet a need in the community and thus lead to more people hearing the gospel in your church.

Endowments to thrive on, rather than survive on, are essential to the future of many congregations. Allow people to designate their gift to a variety of long-term options such as (1) giving without any instruction as to how the money can be used; (2) giving with only the interest to be used, designated or undesignated; (3) giving with both the principal and interest to be used; (4) giving money to be used only for building or maintenance; or (5) giving money to be used only to establish or sustain a ministry or staff person.

Use the endowment to help you thrive instead of just survive. Use it in a way that secures the future of the church's ministry. It is not a matter of whether it is used for capital improvements or whether it is used for programs. It should be used so that it doesn't become a crutch. Place the responsibility for the endowment ministry with a group concerned with ministry instead of with the trustees. This way the people will understand that the money can be used for a variety of ministries, not just for buildings. Too many churches have enough money set aside for the buildings to be taken care of long after all the people are gone.

Question 28: When was our last capital fund drive?

In a growing church, capital fund drives can be done every three years.

Question 29: Does our pastor or someone on the paid staff know what each member gives?

The issue here is that no one should be in leadership who is not doing his or her part with all areas of life, including money. Nontraditional churches understand the need for accountability; traditional churches often struggle with this one. Either they don't trust one another or they are afraid they might lose members if they are open about the money.

Action Items for Asking for Money

1. Involve one-third of the church in the leadership of stewardship education before the actual drive.
2. Change your stewardship year from a calendar year to April through March or May through April.
3. Begin an endowment ministry.
4. Set a goal of receiving 3.5 to 5 percent of the average member's household income by talking about tithing and "stepping up to tithing."
5. Nontraditional churches should never be afraid of raising the bar when it comes to teaching their people to tithe.

Growth Principle 18: Regular Strategic Mapping Must Be Done for Growth to Be Healthy (Key Question: 1)

Data Source: Staff Survey (D:\Surveys\Staff\Staff.doc), questions 159-161; Official Body Survey Totals Spreadsheet (D:\Spreadsheets\Body Survey-Totals Spreadsheet.xls), questions 69-72.

Question 1: Do we have a clear mission statement?

Perhaps the most important thing a church can do is to understand why it exists and how it is going to live out its ministry. There are three types of statements a church needs to make in order to clarify its reason for existence. The *mission statement* is the basic, bottom-line mission of the church. It is why the church exists. It is what keeps the leaders and various teams in alignment. The more diverse the ministries of the church, the more important the mission statement is. It is seldom longer than a sentence, is easily memorized, and is general in nature. The *vision statement* is the narrowly defined mission of the church. It is slightly longer and much more specific than the mission statement. It steers individuals and teams in the direction a particular body is going and what it hopes to accomplish. A church must be clear about its bottom line in order to develop mission and vision statements. The *value statement* sets the boundaries of opportunity in which individuals and groups within the congregation can live out the above two statements without having to get permission to act. It provides the subtle boundaries that informally sanction or prohibit behavior.

The following are the mission, vision, value, and bedrock belief statements for Easum, Bandy & Associates. I have used our statements as examples only because we are not a church and our statement will not directly influence you as you develop your own statements.

Mission: Guiding Christian leaders for ancient mission in the contemporary world.

Vision: To prepare congregations and faith-based organizations for mission in the twenty-first century by training innovative leaders with a passion to grow disciples of Christ, and by providing resources, services, and networks to equip faithful and effective Christian ministries.

Core Values: Embedded and modeled in every member of EBA.

- Teams . . . instead of committees
- Accountability . . . instead of control
- Servanthood . . . instead of hierarchy
- Risk-taking discipleship . . . instead of institutional membership
- Networks and alliances . . . instead of bureaucracy
- Respect for Creator, creature, and creation
- Constant spiritual growth
- Equal emphasis on evangelism, social justice, and Christian nurture

Bedrock Beliefs: Affirmed and articulated by every member of EBA.

- Jesus, fully human and fully divine, is the irrational mystery of faith that beckons all creation into living relationship with God.

- All that matters is the gospel.
- Become all things to all people, that by all means some may be rescued (see 1 Corinthians 9:22)

Action Items for Laying a Solid Foundation

Develop your mission, vision, and value statements if you have not done so already. I've found the following questions helpful in developing a vision and mission statement:

- Will our church focus ministry primarily on the needs within our congregation or will we focus as much attention on the needs of the unchurched in the community as we do on ourselves?
- Can a church be a church without concerning itself about the unchurched around it?
- Are we going to be a church that depends mostly on the pastor for congregational care and evangelistic outreach or are we going to develop a laity-driven ministry that incorporates both pastoral care and evangelistic outreach?
- Are we going to be a program-based church that invites people to attend programs led by a professional staff, or are we going to be a small-group-based church that relies less on program and staff and more on the priesthood of the believers and the networking between members and their friends outside the church?
- Are we going to be basically a Sunday church or are we going to be a seven-day-a-week church? And if so what are our core ministries during the week?
- Will all of our ministries be conducted on the church property, or will we develop satellite ministries?
- Are we content with developing worship designed basically for people who are over fifty or who may be under fifty but have never left the church? Or are we going to also provide worship designed for people especially in their twenties and thirties who have left the church?
- What does Acts say about the role of stewardship of money in our lives, and are we living up to the New Testament understanding of tithing?
- Are we willing to add staff members to the church in order to reach the unchurched, or will we remain staffed as we are?

Three excellent resources for exploring these questions are *Moving Off the Map* by Thomas G. Bandy, *Unfreezing Moves* by Bill Easum, and *The Path* by Lauri Beth Jones.

The ability of your church to reach the unchurched people in your community depends largely on how you decide to answer the above questions.

It might also be helpful to review the essential pieces of the New Testament church: it is biblically grounded, is culturally relevant, exists to transform and disciple, mobilizes the congregation for mission, and is a community built on trust.

Growth Principle 19: It Takes More Effort to Implement Change than to Maintain the Status Quo or to Exercise Veto Power (Key Questions: 1-7)

Data Source: Staff Survey (D:\Surveys\Staff\Staff.doc), questions 162-164; Official Body Survey Totals Spreadsheet (D:\Spreadsheets\Body Survey-Totals Spreadsheet.xls), questions 73-76; Worship Survey Totals Spreadsheet (D:\Spreadsheets\Worship Survey-Totals Spreadsheet.xls), questions 12-14.

Questions 1, 2: Is our church free from power cliques?

Every church has power cliques; however, the more powerful that the cliques become, the less capable of moving forward the church will be. When one or two people have the ability to sway the direction of a vote, this inhibits the church's growth. The best thing you can do is to quit listening to the negative power cliques. If you determine a handful of people are derailing the wishes of the majority, confront them with the information, and either correct the situation or ask them to leave.

Questions 3, 4: How long have we been members?

In traditional churches the longer that leaders have been members of the church, the less likely they will understand the hurts and hopes of those who have never been inside a church. If the average leader filling out the Ministry Audit is over forty-five years of age and has been a member for more than five years, it is highly important that you do focus groups with people under forty-five years of age who do not go to church in order to gain insights into who they are and how to reach them.

Questions 5, 6: How many participated in the audit?

The more people who fill out the Official Body Survey, the more accurate it will be. If you have a small cadre of leaders fill it out and the scores are high, be sure and check to see if one or two of the group answered eight, nine, or ten on many of the questions.

Question 7: Do we make summer schedule changes?

The only changes that should be made in the summer are adding ministries. For example, offer an outdoor worship service or plan more youth activities. Avoid combining worship services, changing the times, or dropping Sunday school. Cutting back in the summer is planning for a summer slump and makes the fall that much harder. Traditional churches are the worst offenders here. It is rare to find a thriving church that cuts back in the summer.

Action Items for Making Changes

1. Identify the power cliques and address the problem if they are too powerful. Matthew 18 is a good example of what disciples should aspire to be.
2. Do not reduce the schedules in the summer; instead, add to the choices.
3. As an indicator of ability to change, see the comments on the totals for the Staff and Official Body Readiness Surveys in section 3. (Hint: Use the files on the CD-ROM to compile the survey results and easily obtain these totals.)
4. In order to get an indication of how much power is given to cliques, even at the top, see the comments on how to interpret the Staff and Official Body Permission Giving Totals in section 3. (Hint: Use the files on the CD-ROM to compile the survey results and easily obtain these totals.)

Section Six

After The Study

The Report

Make a Diagnosis

In making this report, remember you are functioning more as a physician making a diagnosis and then writing a prescription. Neither is a value judgment, but is as accurate a reading of the church's condition and recommended course of action as possible.

Make measured, dated, and simple recommendations or trigger points to the official body of your church. I do not recommend that you do this study and then fail to make some form of definite plan of action. Here are two examples.

- Measurable recommendation: Within a year, establish a contemporary service during the church school hour that uses very little liturgy, stresses praise choruses, and uses keyboards and drums.

- Trigger Point: When our largest worship service reaches 80 percent capacity, it is time to begin planning for a third worship service during the Sunday school hour.

Make the Presentation to the Official Body

Charts are essential. Following are examples of types of charts that would be helpful when making your presentation to the official body.

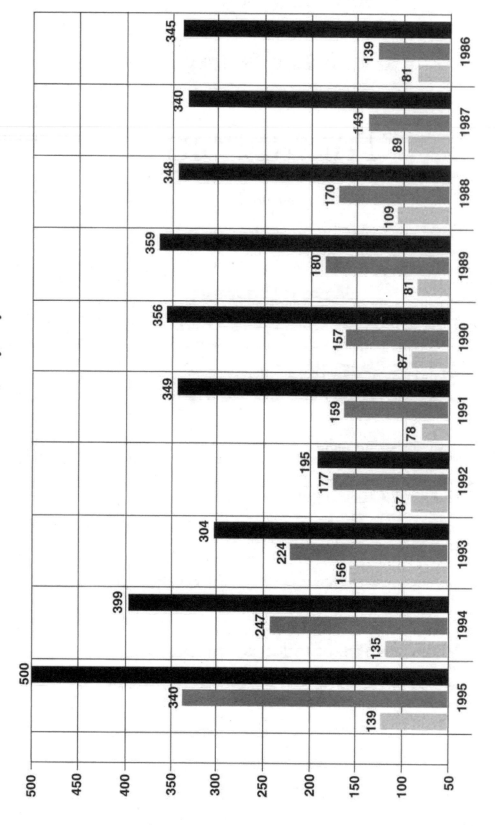

MEMBERSHIP/ATTENDANCE
X Church, Any City

Membership

Worship Attendance

Sunday School Attendance

Year	Membership	Worship Attendance	Sunday School Attendance
1986	345	139	81
1987	340	143	89
1988	348	170	109
1989	359	180	81
1990	356	157	87
1991	349	159	78
1992	195	177	87
1993	304	224	156
1994	399	247	135
1995	500	340	139

AGE OF WORSHIPERS
X Church, Any City

BORN 1946-1964
(65.3%)

BORN 1965-1982 (16.8%)

BORN 1900-1924 (3.0%)

BORN 1925-1945 (14.9%)

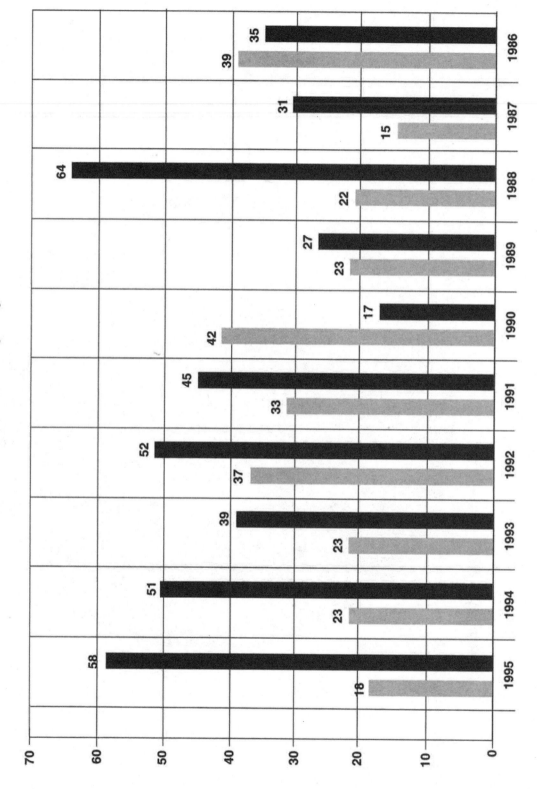

NEW MEMBERS/LOSSES
X Church, Any City

Losses

New Members

READINESS CHART
X Church, Any City

RESISTANT TO GROWTH

READY FOR GROWTH

Y-axis: 10, 9, 8, 7, 6, 5, 4, 3, 2, 1, 0

Category	Official Body (■)	Staff (▲)
Nursery	5.7	1.0
Turf	4.5	1.5
Facilities	1.3	1.0
Reach	1.3	1.0
Change	3.9	1.5
Procedure	5.0	2.5
Debt	7.5	2.5
Spending	5.5	1.0
Worship	1.9	1.0
Attention	3.6	1.0
Staff	2.1	1.0
Trust	2.3	1.0

■ · · · · Official Body   - - ▲ - - Staff

Give a completed copy of the Ministry Audit to all church leaders prior to any meeting regarding the report.

Have several or all of the steering team make portions of the presentation.

Avoid using too many statistics, especially in discussing the demographics.

Never vote on an issue the *first* time you meet to discuss it.

Meet from 7:00 to 9:00 in the evening with no break. Make sure the nursery is open and staffed so that the younger members can attend.

Always begin with a few very positive statements about the church.

Tell those to whom you are presenting the report that you are going to share with them what they have taught you about their church.

Step 1: Introduce the Report

1. Begin by praising the official body for one or two things, especially for the foresight in doing this audit.
2. Move quickly to a time of spiritual reflection. This is a time of motivation. You might want to use some of the material about a faithful, biblical church in Section 1. Make reference to one or more Bible passages (see "The Basic Law of Congregational Life") and be sure to ground your time in solid theology. This time needs to be as much a revival as a lecture about their church and community.
3. Push the official body to think outward rather than inward. You want the focus to be on the community more than the church.
4. Drop hints about the things that are hindering growth. Use humor when possible.

Step 2: Present Your Findings

1. Familiarize the official body with the Ministry Audit but do not go over the audit piece by piece. Use only what is important to your church.
2. Make sure the official body understands how the Ministry Audit was put together. Stress the amount of time involved in collecting the data.
3. Hit the high points.
4. Use graphs or charts. The more visual aids the better. If you are going to use visual aids, you will need an overhead projector and screen. Make sure the words on the transparencies are large enough to be read from the back of the room. The fewer words the better.
5. Avoid being technical or too statistical.
6. Explain each of the nineteen principles that is relevant to your particular church.
7. If you ordered the demographic report from Percept, be sure to share the information that is pertinent, but be careful not to give them too much data. Round off the data. Don't say 33.4 percent; instead just say about one–third.

Step 3: Present Your Recommendations

1. Hand out your recommendations in written form.
2. Make sure everyone understands that these recommendations are the groundwork for future dialogue and decision.
3. Go over the recommendations and let the people ask questions. Avoid defending or arguing the recommendations.

Step 4: Conclude the Report

1. Close with some inspirational story that brings together all the pieces.
2. Leave time to turn the proceedings over to the pastor to close the meeting.

3. Arrange an appropriate closing ahead of time with the pastor.
4. Always make sure that the next step in the process is set in place before the meeting adjourns.

Choose a Process for Moving the Report from Recommendation to Implementation

Your report must be processed through the congregation and revised and refined as you go if it is to reflect the values of the leadership and have a chance of being implemented. Spend all the time necessary to process the material, but remember that there is a limit to the enthusiasm any large group will give to a process before they begin to lose interest. As you go further into the process, more and more of the congregation should have the opportunity to be involved. You will find an example of one process that Bill Easum used through much of his ministry in his book *Sacred Cows Make Gourmet Burgers,* especially in chapter 11.

It is absolutely essential that the key leaders feel good about the recommendations and are willing to share their enthusiasm with the congregation. They must be willing to interpret the recommendations and stand up for them if any opposition arises.

The leadership needs to understand that any time a church attempts to do anything important or to make the strategic adjustments necessary to meet the demands of a new generation, it usually has a few members who strongly oppose such change, if for no other reason than "we have never done it that way before." To give in to these vocal few results in hurting many unseen people by not ministering to their needs. Some people will get upset about your recommendations. That is the case in the vast majority of congregations. Do your best to bring them along in your planning and decision making, but do not allow such opposition to stop the momentum. By the time you finish the process described in *Sacred Cows Make Gourmet Burgers,* the vast majority of the leaders of your church will be ready to move positively on all the amended recommendations. May God bless your efforts as you seek to respond faithfully to the human and spiritual needs around your church and throughout the world.

If you would like Bill Easum to analyze your Ministry Audit, he will do so (for a fee). Reach him by phone at (512) 749-5364; by fax at (512) 749-5800; by e-mail at easum@easumbandy.com; or visit the Web site at www.easumbandy.com.

APPENDIX 1
RESOURCES

Since quality resources are being developed almost continually, rather than include the resources in this book, we decided to include them on our Web site, where we update them on a monthly basis.

Simply go to www.easumbandy.com and click Free Resources and then FAQs. From there you will see a world of resources for any and every thing that you might need to complete the Ministry Audit.

APPENDIX 2
Using the Bonus CD-ROM

Introduction

The electronic materials included with this book have been developed to save you, the end user, time, money, and effort. They have been designed to be user-friendly and to enable your church to quickly and professionally distribute the surveys and compile the results to support the Complete Ministry Audit (CMA).

Benefits of Electronic Materials

There are four main benefits of using the electronic materials on the bonus CD-ROM. The first is that all of the survey templates have been professionally designed to be easy to use and understand, to be pleasing to the eye, and to give people clear and concise information about how to fill out the surveys. This will help you run a smooth survey process for collecting the information for the CMA.

The second benefit is the ease of compiling the survey information and generating the summary statistics necessary to interpret the results. Not only will the enclosed spreadsheets figure out the numerical answers that you need to evaluate your ministry, they'll also help you to prevent making data entry errors.

As a third major benefit, the spreadsheets contain preformatted graphics in full color that simplify looking at the data and understanding the survey results. These graphics will format automatically as data are entered. All you have to do is print them. (They also print out fine on a black and white printer!)

The fourth major benefit of the bonus CD-ROM is that it contains templates for all nineteen Growth Principles. Each question in each Growth Principle contains a reference to the source question in the surveys. This allows for easy reference to the surveys and spreadsheets to find the answers, which can then easily be entered into the Growth Principle files.

The Rest of This Chapter

The remaining portions of this chapter will answer the following questions.

- What are the minimum system requirements necessary to use the electronic materials?
- What are the capabilities of the electronic materials?
- What files are included on the CD-ROM?
- How do I use the templates to make surveys for my church?
- How do I use the spreadsheets to enter in data and total all of the survey information?
- How do I print the graphics in the spreadsheets?
- How do I use the Growth Principle files in support of the CMA?

Please note that in order to best illustrate the above topics, a large number of figures have been included in the text of this chapter. As much as possible, the figures will directly follow the text that referenced them, although in some cases, figures may appear on the next page.

This chapter does not explain how to interpret the results of the surveys. To address that need, please read the previous chapters of this book.

System Requirements

The documents in this bonus CD-ROM have been designed to operate under Microsoft Office® 97 and higher versions. Specifically, the required programs are:

• Microsoft Word® 97 or higher
• Microsoft Excel® 97 or higher

The electronic materials have been tested with all later versions of the above Microsoft Office® programs and found to be compatible.

Microsoft Office® 97 was designed to run on personal computers with the following *minimum* specifications.

• Personal or multimedia computer with a 486 or higher processor
• Microsoft Windows® 95 operating system or later
• 16 MB of RAM
• CD-ROM drive
• VGA or higher-resolution video adapter

Please note that substantial performance enhancements will be achieved by using computers with specifications that exceed the minimum requirements. The recommended specifications include:

• Personal or multimedia computer with a Pentium® II processor or higher
• Microsoft Windows® 2000 operating system or later
• 128 MB of RAM
• CD-ROM drive
• SVGA or higher-resolution video adapter

The complete set of documents in this bonus CD-ROM will occupy less than 30 MB of disk space. This storage amount accounts for all template files and the spreadsheets after data entry is complete.

Understanding the Directory Structure and Files on the Bonus CD-ROM

Figure 1 shows the directory structure of the bonus CD-ROM. There are three top-level folders. The first folder, called "Growth Principles," contains Microsoft Word® files for the nineteen Growth Principles upon which the Complete Ministry Audit is based.

The second folder, called "Spreadsheets," contains all of the spreadsheets for doing the data entry and determining the statistics associated with each survey.

Figure 1. CD Directory Structure

The third top-level folder, called "Surveys," contains three sub-folders. Each sub-folder is labeled with the type of surveys it contains: Body, Staff, or Worship.

Within the directory called "Spreadsheets" there are four files as illustrated in figure 2.

Files Currently on the CD

[x] Body Survey-Totals Spreadsheet.xls

[x] Permission Giving Survey-Totals Spreadsheet.xls

[x] Readiness Survey-Totals Spreadsheet.xls

[x] Worship Survey-Totals Spreadsheet.xls

Figure 2. Spreadsheet Directory Files

Each file is the spreadsheet that will be used for data entry and to generate the summary statistic for a particular survey used in the Complete Ministry Audit. For example, the file called "Body Survey-Totals Spreadsheet.xls" allows you to enter the survey responses to the survey provided to the church body. Later sections of this chapter will go over the data entry requirements for each spreadsheet and survey.

Within each subfolder of the "Survey" directory, you will find several files, as shown in figure 3. Each of the survey files is a stand-alone Word document. Later sections of this chapter will go over how to get each survey ready for distribution.

Name	Size	Type	Date Modified
Files Currently on the CD			
Body.doc	221 KB	Microsoft Word Doc...	9/19/2004 4:20 PM
Body-Permission.doc	85 KB	Microsoft Word Doc...	6/3/2004 12:00 AM
Body-Readiness.doc	65 KB	Microsoft Word Doc...	6/3/2004 12:00 AM

Figure 3. Body Directory Survey Files

Getting Ready to Use the Bonus CD-ROM Files

Prior to using the files on the bonus CD-ROM, it would be best to copy them to the local hard drive of the computer. This will provide you with faster access to the files, allow you to save changes, and preserve the CD-ROM as a backup.

To copy the files, you should first create a folder on the local hard drive. The specific conventions of doing this vary by operating systems. Please refer to the user's guide of your operating system if you are not familiar with the process of creating a new folder.

Once you have created a new folder, you should insert the bonus CD-ROM into your computer's CD-ROM drive and access it. Select all of the directories ("Growth Principles," "Spreadsheets," and "Surveys") and perform a standard COPY command.

Navigate to the new folder on the local hard drive and perform a standard PASTE command. The files will now be copied to the local hard drive where they can safely and easily be used. Please refer to the user's guide of your operating system if you are not familiar with the COPY and PASTE commands.

Getting the Surveys Ready for Distribution

Background Information

Each survey necessary for the CMA is included on the CD-ROM. As explained in a previous section, the surveys are contained in a folder called "Surveys" on the CD-ROM. There are three subfolders labeled:

• Staff
• Body
• Worship

The "Staff" subfolder contains the Permission Giving Survey, the Readiness Survey, and the Staff Survey.

The "Body" subfolder contains the Permission Giving Survey, the Readiness Survey, and the Body Survey.

The "Worship" sub-folder contains a survey form for each week that you will do the congregational survey, labeled as "Week 1" through "Week 4."

All of the surveys contain common elements, such as a logo, a title block that identifies the survey and provides brief instructions, and a footer that informs users that the survey is part of the Complete Ministry Audit. These common elements are important elements in providing you with professional survey handouts to use in your assessment. Best of all, the modifications you need to make are very simple and can be done in just a few minutes.

Templates

Each survey has been created and stored as a Word template. This means that most of the document is "locked" and can't be changed. This was done merely to provide some protection for you when modifying the files. If you are an experienced user and wish to unlock the template files to make further modifications, you are free to do so. The templates are not password protected.

Changing the Title Block In a Survey

Let's see how to use the template to get a survey ready for distribution. Access the directory structure where you copied the files from the CD-ROM. Select the "Surveys" folder and then the "Body" subfolder. Open the file called "Body-Readiness.doc."

The file will open in whatever version of Microsoft Word® you have on your computer. You will see a screen similar to figure 4.

Complete Ministry Audit	**Your Church Name - Official Body Readiness Survey**
	January 1, 2000
	Instructions: Decide how you <u>feel</u> about the following statements, rating your agreement or disagreement with each statement on a scale of one to ten. One (1) means that you totally AGREE with the statement; ten (10) means that you totally DISAGREE with the statement. *PLEASE NOTE THAT THESE SURVEYS ARE COMPLETELY ANONYMOUS AND CONFIDENTIAL*

1. The nursery should be extra clean and neat, staffed with paid help, and open every time there is a church function.
   1   2   3   4   5   6   7   8   9   10

2. Turf issues are harmful to the growth of a church.
   1   2   3   4   5   6   7   8   9   10

3. I am willing for the facilities to be used even if they get dirty.
   1   2   3   4   5   6   7   8   9   10

4. Reaching out to new members is just as important as taking care of the present members.
   1   2   3   4   5   6   7   8   9   10

5. I am comfortable with radical change if it will help my church reach more people for Christ.
   1   2   3   4   5   6   7   8   9   10

6. I am seldom concerned about procedure.
   1   2   3   4   5   6   7   8   9   10

7. Paying off the debt is not a major concern to me.
   1   2   3   4   5   6   7   8   9   10

8. I support the idea of spending some of the church's savings in order to hire more staff or start new programs.
   1   2   3   4   5   6   7   8   9   10

9. Several worship services are fine with me because I am more interested in meeting the needs of all the people than I am in knowing everyone at church.
   1   2   3   4   5   6   7   8   9   10

10. I'm not at all offended when my pastor does not give me regular personal attention.
   1   2   3   4   5   6   7   8   9   10

Figure 4. Body Readiness Survey

Note that in the title block, there are two selections that are colored with either gray or black shading. These are called fields. Fields allow you to safely update certain information in a document without altering any of the rest of the document. When you open a locked template in Word, the program automatically highlights the first field for you, which is why it appears in the darker (black) shading. Please note that the shading only occurs on-screen in Word, and does not appear on the printed form.

To change a field, simply move your mouse over the field and click. This will select the field and give you the standard Word cursor. You can select any spot in the field, but as a hint, it is generally easier to select a spot at the beginning or ending of the field, since the first task you have to do is delete the text that is currently in the field.

Select the field containing the text "Your Church Name" by clicking in the field. Backspace or delete that text. When you have successfully deleted the text in the field, the field will be empty, but still gray.

Go ahead and type in the name of your church. For the purposes of illustrating this concept here, we've elected to use the name "Main Street Church." Figure 5 through figure 7 show the process described above.

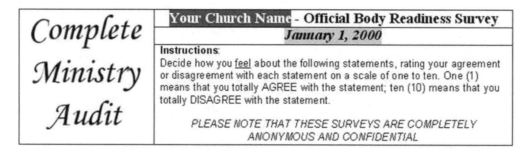

Figure 5. Body Readiness Survey Title Block

Figure 6. Empty Title Block Field

Figure 7. Your Church Name in Title Block

150

Once you've changed the church name, repeat the same process with the field containing the date. Having a field for the date simply allows you to mark the start of the survey period. Figure 8 shows the title block with all the changes completed.

Complete Ministry Audit	Main Street Church - Official Body Readiness Survey
	January 9, 2005
	Instructions: Decide how you <u>feel</u> about the following statements, rating your agreement or disagreement with each statement on a scale of one to ten. One (1) means that you totally AGREE with the statement; ten (10) means that you totally DISAGREE with the statement. *PLEASE NOTE THAT THESE SURVEYS ARE COMPLETELY ANONYMOUS AND CONFIDENTIAL*

Figure 8. Title Block with Completed Changes

Once you have completed the changes to the title block, you are now ready to print the survey. As with any Word document, you can use the printer icon on the toolbar, or go through the menus (File, Print) to print the document.

When you have completed printing the document, note that on the printed copy, the fields are not highlighted. Please remember to save the revised survey (using the toolbar icon or File, Save).

That's all there is to it! Simply repeat the above steps with the other surveys to change their title blocks, save the documents, print them, and you have all of your surveys ready for distribution.

Worship Survey Title Block

Please note that the date field for the worship survey also includes the words "Week 1," "Week 2," "Week 3," or "Week 4." This was done simply to let the congregation know which week of the survey they are in and serves as a reminder for them to participate in the other weeks.

Note to Advanced Users

If you are an advanced user and wish to use your own church logo in the surveys, please feel free to do so. You will have to unlock the template, delete the existing logo, and then insert your logo in the same place. Prior to placing your logo in the document, you should size it to 160 x 160 pixels. Once you have inserted the logo, lock the template, save it, and you will have surveys that are branded to your particular church.

Please note that Easum, Bandy & Associates cannot offer technical assistance on graphic formats, resizing logos, or the process of inserting logos in the survey forms.

Using the Spreadsheets

Using the spreadsheets on the enclosed CD-ROM will save you hours of effort. Even in a small church, the CMA generates several thousand data points. While the surveys provide a rich source of data to assess your ministry, the spreadsheets provide an easy-to-use data entry and analysis system to minimize the time spent entering data and maximize the information you can obtain from it.

Background

The enclosed CD-ROM contains four spreadsheets with the following names:

- Body Survey-Totals Spreadsheet.xls
- Permission Giving Survey-Totals Spreadsheet.xls
- Readiness Survey-Totals Spreadsheet.xls
- Worship Survey-Totals Spreadsheet.xls

Each spreadsheet of course totals the information from the survey for which it is named. For example, the file named "Permission Giving Survey-Totals spreadsheet.xls" is the spreadsheet used to enter the results of all of the Permission Giving Surveys administered during the course of the CMA.

Together, these spreadsheets provide a place to enter the data from virtually every survey response. The only responses that cannot be tallied in a spreadsheet format are the staff survey responses, since they are text-based. Once the data is entered, the spreadsheets will provide summary statistics and graphics that can easily be printed for a wider audience.

Elements Common to All Spreadsheets

Before getting started with any given spreadsheet, it will benefit you to take a few minutes and familiarize yourself with the common elements in all of the spreadsheets. The common elements discussed below all have been designed to provide you with a high level of direction, visual cues, and comfort in working with the electronic files. For some of you who may be new to spreadsheets, never fear. These files are exceptionally user-friendly!

Menu

Figure 9 shows a sample menu from the spreadsheets. The first thing to notice is that each spreadsheet contains multiple sections or "worksheets." Each worksheet is set up for a single task. In the example of figure 9, you will see seven worksheets listed. Clicking any of the worksheet names will take you to that section of the spreadsheet.

Worksheet	Description	Type
Menu	This Spreadsheet's Menu System	Menu
Instructions	Instructions for Using This Spreadsheet	Instructions
Official Body-Readiness	Readiness Survey - Body Data Entry Form	Data Entry
Staff-Readiness	Readiness Survey - Staff Data Entry Form	Data Entry
Readiness Comparison	Church Demographics - Official Body vs Staff	Graphics - **Ready to Print**
Body-National Readiness	Church Demographics - Official Body vs. National Avg.	Graphics - **Ready to Print**
Staff-National Readiness	Church Demographics - Staff vs. National Avg.	Graphics - **Ready to Print**

Figure 9. Sample Spreadsheet Menu

For example, when you click the worksheet name of "Instructions," you'll be presented with a screen similar to figure 10.

FOR YOUR OWN PROTECTION, PLEASE DO NOT, CHANGE THE FORMULAS OR FORMATTING OF THIS SPREADSHEET.	REFER TO THE TEXT OF '*THE COMPLETE MINISTRY AUDIT*' FOR COMPLETE INSTRUCTIONS ON THE USE OF THIS SPREADSHEET.
Instruction	
The menuing system and the tabs at the bottom of this spreadsheet allow for easy navigation.	
Each worksheet has an easy link back to the menu in the upper left hand corner.	
This spreadsheet contains data entry areas and charts for the Readiness Survey from the Complete Ministry Audit.	
Before starting, randomly shuffle all returned survey, then number them, starting at 1. Write the number on the first sheet of the survey. This enables us to go back to any survey to find a particular answer in the case of a data entry mistake	
Use the menu to go the data entry area for the Official Body.	
Using the on-screen help boxes, expand the "+" sign above Column CX to enter in data from the Official Body.	
There is space for entering results from 100 surveys. Each column represents one survey. Each row is one question.	
Automatic formatting is in use to help you catch data entry errors. Values can only be between 1 and 10. The cell will turn light blue if the data is entered correctly.	
The value in the cell will turn **bright red** if the value you entered was **too low**.	
The value in the cell will turn **bright purple** if the value you entered was **too high**.	
Use the on-screen comments and the instructions in the manual to help with finding any data entry errors.	
The spreadsheet will automatically calculate the average of all the responses and report that figure in Column DX.	
Once you have completed the data entry for the Official Body Readiness Surveys, repeat the same steps for the Staff Readiness Surveys.	
Once all of the data entry is completed, use the menuing system to go to any chart.	
Following the on-screen comments on the chart pages, click once in the chart to select hit, then hit the printer icon on the toolbar, or select File, Print from the menu.	

Figure 10. Sample Instructions

Note that every worksheet has a line labeled "Return to Menu" in the upper-left-hand corner of the screen. Clicking this link will always return you to the main menu, located in the first worksheet. You will not lose any information or data by moving around the spreadsheet to the different sections. This menu capability is provided simply to help improve the efficiency of working with large spreadsheets.

You'll also notice a few other things about the menu in figure 9. One is that each worksheet also contains a brief description of what it does and there's also a color-coded notation of what category the worksheet falls in.

Across all of the spreadsheets contained in the CD-ROM, the colors and menu systems have been kept consistent. Gray will always be a menu. Red is always an instruction page, containing information specific to that particular spreadsheet. Orange is always a data entry worksheet, where you will actually enter in the responses from surveys. Green is always a table of statistics compiled from the survey results. Finally, blue is always a graphic output—all you have to do is click and print.

Tabs

Excel also provides another method of moving around spreadsheets. Known as tabs, each spreadsheet has multiple links at the bottom of the screen. The idea of tabs is exactly analogous to multiple files in a folder. You write the name of each file on the tab, which allows you to quickly find what you want. Figure 11 shows an example of tabs in the spreadsheets for the Complete Ministry Audit.

| ◄ ◄ ► ►◄ \ Menu / Instructions / Official Body-Readiness / Staff-Readiness / Readiness Comparison / Body-National Readiness / Staff-National Readiness |

Figure 11. Tabs in Spreadsheet

Note that the tabs have been color-coded exactly like the menu. Although the tabs cannot provide you with the full set of information like the menu will, they are a perfectly acceptable method of moving around a spreadsheet. In fact, you can use the menu to move to one worksheet, return to the menu as detailed above, and use the menu to move to another worksheet. In the bottom line, it makes no difference how you move around the spreadsheet, merely that you use whatever tools and methods feel most comfortable to you.

Instructions

Each spreadsheet contains a set of instructions, as shown in figure 10. The information contained in the instructions is more general than what is contained in this chapter and is meant to highlight some of the major points to remember when working with the spreadsheets.

The "Worship Survey-Totals Spreadsheet.xls" actually contains two pages of instructions. The first page contains the overall information and the second page contains a graphic detailing how to code each survey response, prior to data entry. This will be covered in detail in a later portion of this chapter.

The Basics of Data Entry

The most important task related to any of the spreadsheets is the entry of the survey results. Careful analysis of these results is the basis for the evaluation of your ministry. To help make the data entry task as easy as possible, the spreadsheets use a few methods to help flag data that is entered incorrectly.

Let's consider an example. A number of the survey questions ask respondents to answer questions on a scale of one to ten. Question 2 from the Permission Giving Survey administered to both the official body and the staff is below.

2. People at the lowest level of organization in our church should be able to suggest and implement improvements to their own ministry without going through several committees and levels of approval.

    1   2   3   4   5   6   7   8   9   10

The instructions in the survey state that a response of one means you completely agree with the statement, while a response of ten means you completely disagree with the statement. Any answer from one to ten is therefore acceptable and valid.

To understand how the data entry works, look at figure 12. This figure shows the data entry section for the official body responses to the Permission Giving Survey.

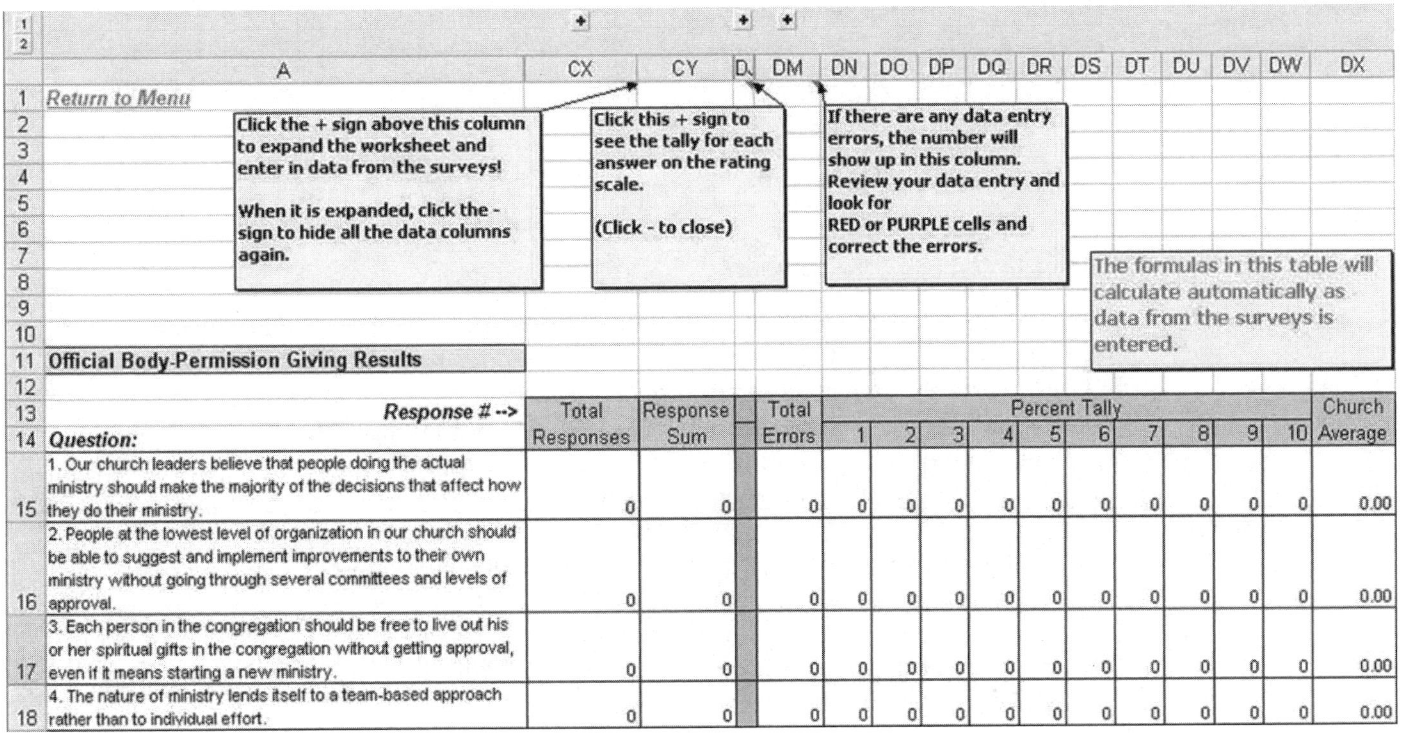

Figure 12. Data Entry Basics

What you should first notice is that the questions in the survey are shown in the leftmost column (column A) of the worksheet. The next column over (column CX) shows the total number of responses to the survey. Currently, that number is "0," as you have not entered any data. You will also see a column that sums or adds all of the responses. The average that is provided in the last column is basic math of the total of all responses divided by the total number of responses. The other columns represent data that will become more apparent as you enter in responses.

What you will also note in figure 12 is a series of notes that contain helpful hints pertaining to the worksheet. The leftmost hint says to click the "+" sign located above column CX to enter in data. Because this worksheet can handle up to one hundred responses to the survey, there are one hundred columns that could be displayed with values from one to ten. That would make it pretty tedious to move around the worksheet easily, so the worksheets utilize a concept called data grouping. All data grouping does is combine a group of columns together and provide an easy way to either hide or display them.

The columns for data entry can easily be accessed by clicking the "+" sign. When the columns are shown, your screen will be similar to figure 13.

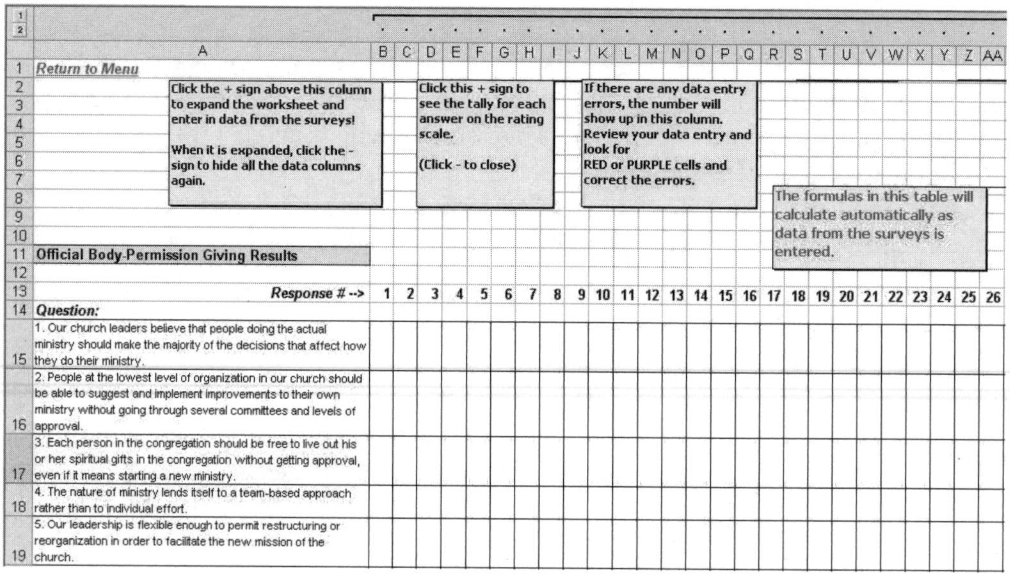

Figure 13. Data Entry Expanded

The number of the survey appears near the top of the screen. This means that a single column represents all of the answers from a single survey. A single row contains all of the answers to a single question.

OK! Let's see how some data entry works! We said before that the worksheets use some techniques to alert you to bad data. In the case of the example question above, allowable answers are one through ten. Bad data would be anything zero and below or anything eleven and above. It's pretty easy to type a "0" instead of a "10" by not hitting a key. Likewise, you can hit a key twice pretty easily and get "11." So the worksheets help to catch some of those common mistakes.

Figure 14 shows a number of responses entered for question 2. Note that in all of the correct responses, the cell gets filled in with a light-blue color. When that happens, you know you've typed a correct response.

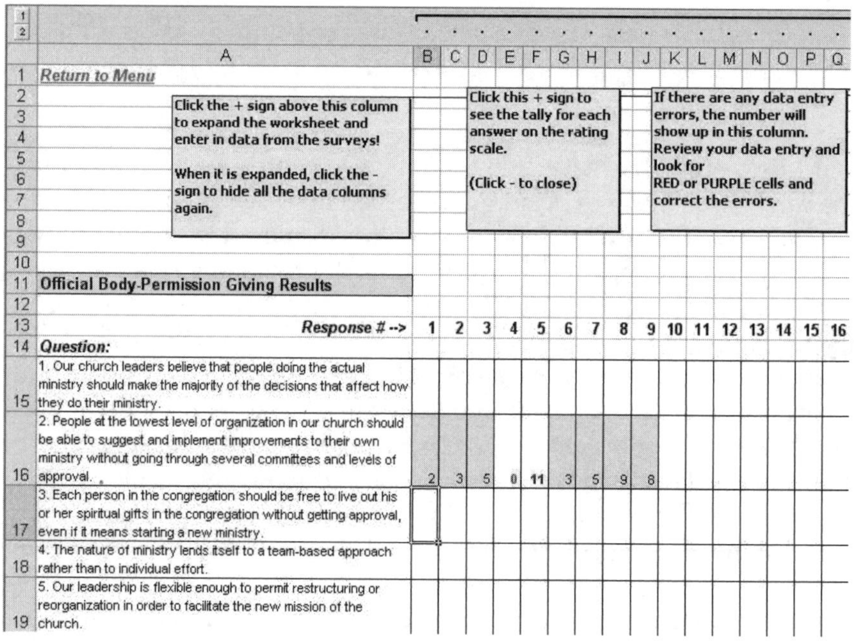

Figure 14. Data Entry Mistakes

If, however, you went to type "10" and typed "0" instead, note that the cell will not turn light blue. Instead, the number you entered will be set in boldface and shown in red. This is to help signal you that there is a mistake in the data entry.

In a very similar manner, if you went to type a "1" and instead typed "11," the number you entered will be set in boldface and shown in purple. Again, this is simply a visual clue to help you pick up data entry errors. When most of the cells on the screen are a light blue, the cells containing bad data become evident very quickly.

Please note that the worksheet cannot catch all data entry errors. For example, suppose the response to a question was a "5" and instead you typed a "4." Since "4" is a valid response, the worksheet will not flag that response as being incorrect. In other words, while the worksheet will catch the obvious data entry errors, you should be careful with data entry to ensure accuracy when entering the survey responses.

When you've finished the data entry and you close the data grouping (by clicking the "-" sign instead of the "+" sign), you'll see that the worksheet has started to calculate some statistics for you. These values will be updated every time you add more data.

Figure 15 shows an example of what the screen would look like with some data entry completed for question 2. Note that since we did *not* correct the data entry errors we saw in figure 14, the worksheet is still telling us that there are two data entry errors, as seen in column DM.

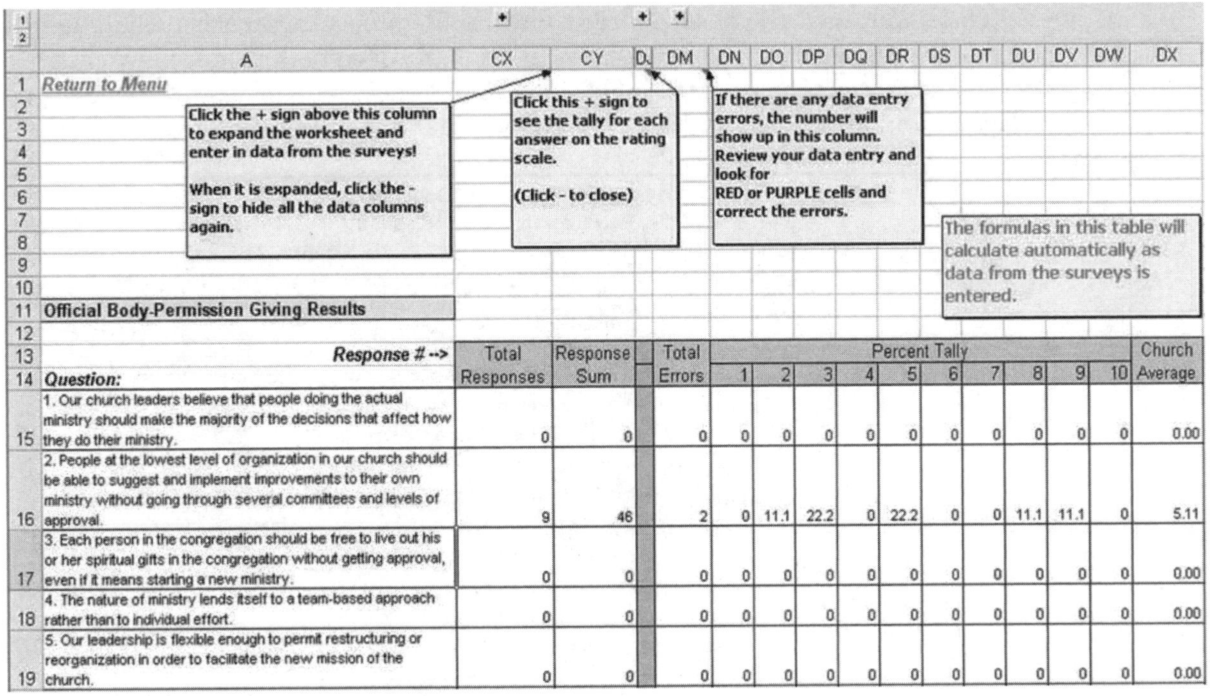

Response # -->	Total Responses	Response Sum	Total Errors	Percent Tally 1	2	3	4	5	6	7	8	9	10	Church Average
Question:														
1. Our church leaders believe that people doing the actual ministry should make the majority of the decisions that affect how they do their ministry.	0	0	0	0	0	0	0	0	0	0	0	0	0	0.00
2. People at the lowest level of organization in our church should be able to suggest and implement improvements to their own ministry without going through several committees and levels of approval.	9	46	2	0	11.1	22.2	0	22.2	0	0	11.1	11.1	0	5.11
3. Each person in the congregation should be free to live out his or her spiritual gifts in the congregation without getting approval, even if it means starting a new ministry.	0	0	0	0	0	0	0	0	0	0	0	0	0	0.00
4. The nature of ministry lends itself to a team-based approach rather than to individual effort.	0	0	0	0	0	0	0	0	0	0	0	0	0	0.00
5. Our leadership is flexible enough to permit restructuring or reorganization in order to facilitate the new mission of the church.	0	0	0	0	0	0	0	0	0	0	0	0	0	0.00

Figure 15. Data Entry Summary

Additionally, you can see in figure 15 that the worksheet has computed the current average from all of the entered responses.

Statistical Results

As detailed above, figure 15 shows how entering survey data will allow the worksheet to compute the average of all the responses. While this is the basic information required for the survey, the worksheet also provides some additional information or statistics.

For example, columns DN through DW will show you the percentage of survey respondents that answered each question with the values one through ten. This can be very informative because it can tell how "spread" the survey responses are. If a large percentage of the surveys are clustered around responses one through three, then a large percentage of the respondents agree with the statement. Likewise, a large percentage of responses clustered around eight, nine, or ten would indicate that a significant percentage of the respondents disagree with the statement.

While analysis of these trends can provide an interesting and insightful look into the church, it is beyond the scope of this text to provide detail on how to do that. However, the worksheets contain and report the data, allowing experienced users the opportunity to gain additional knowledge from the survey response.

Graphical Results

Each of the spreadsheets contains charts that can be printed out. Professionally designed and formatted in full color, the charts can be very effective displays of the vast amount of survey data that you will get from all of the responses.

Each chart in the spreadsheet is linked from the menu, as described in previous sections. Simply click the menu link to go to the appropriate chart. Some spreadsheets contain only a single chart, while others contain multiple charts.

Once you have responses entered into the data entry worksheet, the charts will format automatically. Figure 16 shows an example of a chart produced by entering all of the survey responses from both the official body and staff who responded to the Permission Giving Survey.

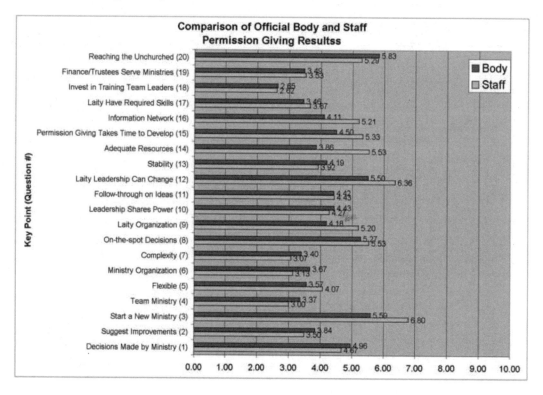

Figure 16. Example of Spreadsheet Chart

Please note that in order to print a chart, it is very important to click anywhere in the chart prior to selecting print from the menu. Clicking inside the chart tells Excel that you want to print only the chart, not the entire worksheet. Each worksheet that contains a chart has a note on the page reminding you to click the chart prior to printing the document.

Notes Specific to Each Spreadsheet

Previous sections of this text have shown you how the spreadsheets are set up, how to move around a spreadsheet, how to enter in data, and also how to print out graphical results.

The following sections describe any information specific to an individual spreadsheet. These sections do not detail the inner workings of each spreadsheet, but they do describe the overall capabilities of the spreadsheet and its relation to the surveys.

Body Survey-Totals Spreadsheet.xls

The Body Survey-Totals Spreadsheet serves as the data entry and analysis package for the Official Body Survey. The Official Body Survey is a series of seventy-six questions that is administered to the official body of the church.

The spreadsheet has been designed to tally the answers from one hundred surveys. This should be flexible enough to handle even the largest churches.

Prior to starting data entry, it is recommended that you randomly sort all of the responses. If anyone has written his or her name on a response, either erase it or mark through it to make it unreadable. Both of these things should be done to help ensure anonymity in the responses.

However, to ensure correct data entry and to track down any errors, you do want to number the surveys after you randomly sort them. Simply assign consecutive numbers, starting with one, in the upper-right-hand corner of each survey. You will then enter all the responses for survey 1 in the column labeled for that response number. In the worksheet for data entry, column B will be for entering survey response 1, column C will be for entering survey response 2, and so on. In this manner, you will be able to easily find any survey response and check the data entry.

As you do the data entry for the Body, Permission Giving, and Readiness surveys, you will note that the spreadsheet will only allow you to enter in values of one through ten. Do not try to enter blank responses as a zero, since this will incorrectly influence the averages.

As a final note for the Official Body Survey, questions 68 through 71 are not tallied numerically. You can tally the answers separately on a sheet of paper.

Permission Giving Survey-Totals Spreadsheet.xls

The Permission Giving Survey-Totals Spreadsheet serves as the data entry and analysis package for the Permission Giving Survey. This survey is a series of twenty questions, answered on a scale of one to ten that is administered to both the official body and the church staff.

The spreadsheet has been designed to handle data entry for up to one hundred responses from the official body and up to one hundred responses from church staff.

As with the other survey responses, steps should be taken to preserve the anonymity of the responses and allow you to track the data entry to help prevent erroneous data. Please refer to the more detailed discussion in the section detailing the Body Survey-Totals Spreadsheet. Additionally, the same note about not entering zero for blank answers applies.

Readiness Survey-Totals Spreadsheet.xls

The Readiness Survey-Totals Spreadsheet serves as the data entry and analysis package for the Readiness Survey. This survey is a series of twelve questions, answered on a scale of one to ten that is administered to both the official body and the church staff.

The spreadsheet has been designed to handle data entry for up to one hundred responses from the official body and up to one hundred responses from church staff.

As with the other survey responses, steps should be taken to preserve the anonymity of the responses and allow you to track the data entry to help prevent erroneous data. Please refer to the more detailed discussion in the section detailing the Body Survey-Totals Spreadsheet. Additionally, the same note about not entering zero for blank answers applies.

Worship Survey-Totals Spreadsheet.xls

While the worship survey is the shortest survey, its use over four weeks to the entire congregation means that it generates more responses than any of the other surveys. For this reason, the data entry and analysis spreadsheet for the worship survey was built to summarize the survey response from the smallest to even the largest congregations.

The spreadsheet can handle five thousand responses for each of the four weeks of the worship survey. It will compute all of the statistics necessary from that data and provide you with preformatted tables and graphics.

There are two special notes about the worship survey. The first pertains to data entry of the survey, while the second pertains to data required by another survey. Each of these special topics is addressed below.

Worship Survey Data Entry

The worship survey is somewhat unique among all of the surveys in the Complete Ministry Audit because its answers are not provided on a scale of one to ten. In fact, if you've looked at the survey, you know that the response to some questions are a geographic direction, a favorite music format, and yes/no answers.

It would be very tedious to type in all of the word responses to these questions. In addition, the spreadsheet would be very prone to errors, since spelling and capitalization would confuse a spreadsheet. For example, although we know that "Yes" and "yes" both mean the same thing, a spreadsheet will see those as different answers. Likewise, the capitalization error of "yEs" and the spelling error of "Yse" would all be seen as different answers, but we know they are really meant to be the same.

They key to getting around this problem is entering the survey responses as numbers, not words. After all, there is only one way to type the number "1"!

So let's look at how we can apply this to the worship survey. Let's take an example question, such as question 2.

2. My gender is: Male   ☐
Please check one   Female   ☐

Let's assign the value of one to the response of "Male" and assign a value of two to "Female." In the data entry, all we then have to do is enter in a one or a two and don't have to worry about any spelling or capitalization problems in typing out the answers in the spreadsheet.

In fact, we can do this for *every* question in the worship survey. The data entry process then becomes a maximum of fourteen numbers to enter, which speeds up how fast you can enter data, in addition to how much more error-free the process becomes. Figure 17 shows a worship survey with all of the "coding" overlaid onto the form.

Randomly shuffle surveys and mark each one sequentially, starting at 1 → **1**

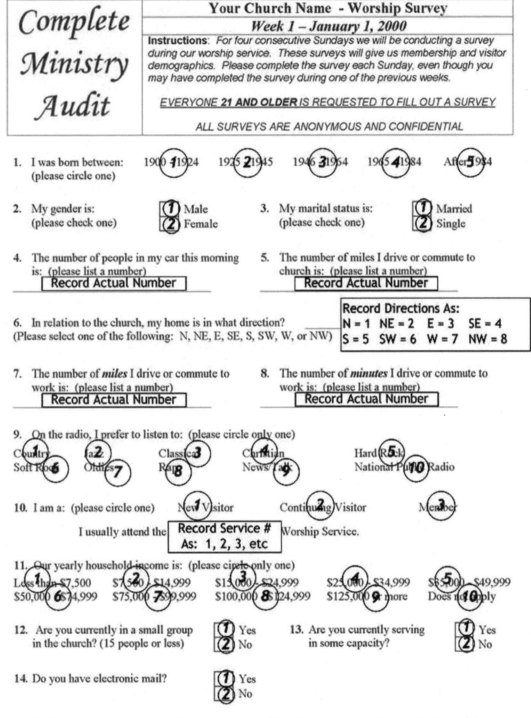

Figure 17. Worship Survey Coding for Data Entry

You can probably understand that it's more efficient and error-free to type in numbers instead of words. However, you may ask yourself how you should apply this to the overall process of entering data for the worship survey.

We recommend that you add a step in the process prior to entering the information into the spreadsheet. Once you've collected the worship surveys, put them all in a pile and sit down at the table. Print out a copy of figure 17 for reference.

Starting with the first survey in the pile, write a number one in the upper-right-hand corner. This is done for the same reason as in the other surveys: allowing you to backtrack to a particular survey if you need to check the data entry.

Starting with question 1, assign the numerical equivalent of the answer to the question. The recommendation is that you actually write a large number across the question, so that there will be no mistake about what value to enter into the spreadsheet. Figure 18 and figure 19 show examples of this whole process.

Figure 18 shows an example survey that was filled out during the worship survey by a respondent. The answers are clearly indicated on the page, with a combination of writing, circles, and "X's." Using figure 17 as the reference sheet for coding the answers, figure 19 shows the result.

Complete *Ministry* *Audit*	**Your Church Name - Worship Survey** ***Week 1 – January 1, 2000*** **Instructions**: *For four consecutive Sundays we will be conducting a survey during our worship service. These surveys will give us membership and visitor demographics. Please complete the survey each Sunday, even though you may have completed the survey during one of the previous weeks.* *EVERYONE **21 AND OLDER** IS REQUESTED TO FILL OUT A SURVEY* *ALL SURVEYS ARE ANONYMOUS AND CONFIDENTIAL*

1. I was born between: 1900 - 1924   1925 - 1945   (1946 - 1964)   1965 - 1984   After 1984
(please circle one)

2. My gender is: [X] Male   3. My marital status is: [X] Married
(please check one)   [ ] Female   (please check one)   [ ] Single

4. The number of people in my car this morning is: (please list a number)   **2**

5. The number of miles I drive or commute to church is: (please list a number)   **5.5**

6. In relation to the church, my home is in what direction?   **N**
(Please select one of the following: N, NE, E, SE, S, SW, W, or NW)

7. The number of *miles* I drive or commute to work is: (please list a number)   **10**

8. The number of *minutes* I drive or commute to work is: (please list a number)   **20**

9. On the radio, I prefer to listen to: (please circle only one)

(Country)   Jazz   Classical   Christian   Hard Rock
Soft Rock   Oldies   Rap   News/Talk   National Public Radio

10. I am a: (please circle one)   New Visitor   (Continuing Visitor)   Member

I usually attend the   **11 AM**   Worship Service.

11. Our yearly household income is: (please circle only one)

Less than $7,500 $7,500 - $14,999 $15,000 - $24,999 $25,000 - $34,999   ($35,000 - $49,999)
$50,000 - $74,999 $75,000 - $99,999 $100,000 - $124,999 $125,000 or more   ~~Does not apply~~

12. Are you currently in a small group in the church? (15 people or less)   [ ] Yes   [X] No

13. Are you currently serving in some capacity?   [ ] Yes   [X] No

14. Do you have electronic mail?   [X] Yes   [ ] No

Figure 18. Worship Survey Example

Complete Ministry Audit	**Your Church Name - Worship Survey**
	Week 1 – January 1, 2000
	Instructions: *For four consecutive Sundays we will be conducting a survey during our worship service. These surveys will give us membership and visitor demographics. Please complete the survey each Sunday, even though you may have completed the survey during one of the previous weeks.*
	*EVERYONE **21 AND OLDER** IS REQUESTED TO FILL OUT A SURVEY*
	ALL SURVEYS ARE ANONYMOUS AND CONFIDENTIAL

1. I was born between: 1900 - 1924   1925 - 1945   (1946 - 1964) **3**   1965 - 1984   After 1984
    (please circle one)

2. My gender is: ☒ **1** Male
    (please check one) ☐ Female

3. My marital status is: ☒ **1** Married
    (please check one) ☐ Single

4. The number of people in my car this morning is: (please list a number)   **2**

5. The number of miles I drive or commute to church is: (please list a number)   **5.5**

6. In relation to the church, my home is in what direction?   **N 1**
(Please select one of the following: N, NE, E, SE, S, SW, W, or NW)

7. The number of *miles* I drive or commute to work is: (please list a number)   **10**

8. The number of *minutes* I drive or commute to work is: (please list a number)   **20**

9. On the radio, I prefer to listen to: (please circle only one)

    (Country) **1**   Jazz   Classical   Christian   Hard Rock
    Soft Rock   Oldies   Rap   News/Talk   National Public Radio

10. I am a: (please circle one)   New Visitor   (Continuing Visitor) **2**   Member

    I usually attend the **3 11 AM** Worship Service.

11. Our yearly household income is: (please circle only one)

    Less than $7,500 $7,500 - $14,999 $15,000 - $24,999 $25,000 - $34,999   ($35,000 - $49,999) **5**
    $50,000 - $74,999 $75,000 - $99,999 $100,000 - $124,999 $125,000 or more   Does not apply

12. Are you currently in a small group in the church? (15 people or less)   ☐ Yes ☒ **2** No

13. Are you currently serving in some capacity?   ☐ Yes ☒ **2** No

14. Do you have electronic mail?   ☒ **1** Yes ☐ No

Figure 19. Worship Survey Example-Coded for Data Entry

Note that question 10 is really a two-part question. The first part asks what type of member the respondent is, while the second part asks what service it is. To assign numbers to your services for the second part of the question, simply take the first service of the week and make it number one. That may be an 8 AM Sunday morning service, as an example. If other services are held at 9:45 AM and 11 AM, those services would then be coded as two and three.

You might be asking yourself if all of this "manipulation" is worth the effort or even necessary. The answer to both questions is *yes*. We've already seen that it is necessary to enter the responses as numbers instead of text, to greatly increase the accuracy of the data entry. Greater accuracy means better results to you, the survey team trying to assess your church! You'll also find as you start to go through the process that while it sounds a little daunting at first, you will get the hang of it very quickly. Ultimately, this process saves quite a bit of time in entering all of the survey responses.

What to Do about Blank Answers?

There are two final notes on the data entry process for the worship survey. The first is that it is very important that you *do not* enter a zero when someone leaves a question blank on a survey response. The reason for this is very simple. Entering a zero will affect the average since it is recorded as a response. Consider the following brief example.

You have three survey responses with the following answers:

Survey 1= 2
Survey 2= 4
Survey 3= Blank

The correct average is $(2 + 4) \div 2$ responses, which equals 3.

If you include the blank response as a zero, the average becomes $(2 + 4 + 0) \div 3$ responses, which equals 2.

So including blank responses as zero will skew your results and give you lower averages than what your results really indicate. If you come across a blank answer, simply treat it as blank and enter nothing into the spreadsheet.

Data Entry for Questions 4, 5, 7, and 8

The second note about the data entry for the worship survey concerns questions 4, 5, 7, and 8. You will note that these questions ask about mileage, time, or number of people in a car. There could be a wide range of possible answers to those questions. You might have a visitor who was in town that weekend write down that he drove one thousand miles to come to church!

For that reason, the worksheets where you enter the data will allow *any* numerical answer for these four questions in the worship survey. Every answer will be treated as a valid response and figured into the average. Because of this, the cells will not turn light blue in the worksheet.

Worship Survey Results for Staff Survey Question 1

The first question in the staff survey asks for a report on the results of the worship survey and tallies the responses with respect to birth year, gender, and marital status. The worship survey totals spreadsheet will tabulate all of this information automatically. The spreadsheet contains a worksheet entitled "Staff Survey-Question 1

Data Table." When the data entry for the worship survey is complete, simply use the menu to go to the data table worksheet and print the results for inclusion with the staff survey.

Using the Growth Principle Templates

In the Complete Ministry Audit, the assessment is conducted on the basis of nineteen principles for church growth. The questions that make up these Growth Principles are not new, since they are all contained in either the body or staff surveys. They simply have to be rearranged in a manner that groups similar questions together to reveal trends and patterns for the analysis.

To make this rearrangement process easier, the bonus CD-ROM provides a Word document for each Growth Principle. Inside each file, you'll find the standard title block that you've seen on the surveys. You'll also see the questions that belong in each Growth Principle.

There are two main types of question formats that you will see. The first is a text-based answer, which typically comes from a question in the staff survey. Figure 20 shows how a typical question will look.

3. What are our people programs, including specialized ministries?
(Source: Staff – Question 2)

Figure 20. Example of Text-Based Growth-Principle Question

The most important item to note is the final line of the box, which will always contain the reference to find the source question. In figure 20, this question came from question 2 in the staff survey. You can go back to the results of the staff survey, find the answer, and type it into the provided space. Alternatively, if you're comfortable working between multiple files, you may find it easier to simply cut and paste the answer from the staff survey question into the growth principle. There are no "rules" for these files. They are simply provided to help make your job of assembling the questions into the Growth Principles as easy as possible.

The second type of question you will see is one that contains a numerical answer. These typically come from the body survey. Figure 21 shows a sample of what a typical question will look like.

2. Our lead pastor understands the everyday world of our members.	
Church Average	
National Average	**2.73**
Deviation	
(Source: Body – Question 1)	

Figure 21. Example of Numerical Growth-Principle Question

There are several items to note for questions like this. First, the question is asking for a numerical response or average. This value will be found in the file titled "Body Survey-Totals Spreadsheet.xls." This is where you have previously entered all of the data from the body survey responses. If you refer to the last line of the box, it will provide a reference to the source question.

In the spreadsheet, click the menu to go to the "Official Body Survey Results." Now, simply find the same question number, find the average result reported in column DX, and record that value back in the Growth Principle file.

Figure 21 also shows a line and corresponding value for the national average. As explained in the text, this value is an average result of surveys performed at more than 250 churches across the United States.

The next line is labeled as "Deviation." The deviation is nothing more than your church average minus the national average. If your church average was 2.00, the deviation would be (2.00 - 2.73) or - 0.73. The negative simply means that your church is below the national average. Likewise, if your church average value was 3.00, the deviation would be (3.00 - 2.73) or + 0.27. Please refer to the text to determine how those deviation values can be interpreted for your church.

As a final helpful hint, table 1 contains a listing of where all of the questions in the nineteen Growth Principles come from. In the table, "S" refers to the Staff Survey, so Growth Principle 4, question 9 comes from S36, or Staff Survey question 36. Likewise, B refers to the Body Survey, so Growth Principle 10, question 6 comes from Body Survey question 39. Remember that the answers to the Body Survey questions will actually be taken from the totals spreadsheet for the Body Survey.

Table 1. Matrix of Growth Principle Questions

Growth Principle

Question	1	2	3	4	5	6	7	8	9	10	11	12	13	14	15	16	17	18	19
1	S1	S8	S26	S28	S37	B4	B17	S47	B25	B38	S77	B58	S93	S100	S106	S118	S133	S159	B73
2	B1	S9	S27	S29		B5	S38	S48	B26	S63	B43	S81	S94	S101	S107	S119	B66	S160	B74
3	S2	S10		S30		B6	S39	S49	S60	S64	S78	B59	S95	S102a	S108	S120	B67	B69	B75
4	S3	S11		S31		B7	S40	S50	S61	S65	B44	S82	S96	S102b	S109	S121	S134	B70	B76
5	B2	S12		S32		B8	S41	S51	S62	S66	B45	S83	S97	S103	S110	S122	S135	B72	S162
6	S4	S13		S33		B9	B18	B23	B27	B39	B46	S84	S98	S104	S111	S123	S136	S161	S163
7	B3	S14		S34		B10	B19	S53	B28	B40	B47	S85	S99	S105	S112	S124	S137		S164
8	S5	S15		S35		B11	B20	B24	B29	S67	B48	S86	B60		S113	B61	B68		
9	S6	S16		S36		B12	B21	S54	B30	S68	B49	S87			S114	S125	S138		
10	S7	S17				B13	B22	S55	B31	S69	B50	S88			S115	S126	S139		
11	S18					B14	S42	S56	B32	S70	B51	S89			S116	B62	S140		
12	S19					B15	S43	S57	B33	S71	B52	S90			S117	B63	S141		
13	S20					B16	S44	S58	B34	S72	B53	S91				S127	S142		
14	S21						S45	S59	B35	B41	B54	S92				S128	S143		
15	S22						S46		B36	B42	B55					B64	S144		
16	S23								B37	S73	B56					B65	S145		
17	S24								S80	S74	B57					S129	S146		
18	S25									S75	S79					S130	S147		
19										S76	S80					S131	S148		
20																S132	S149		
21																	S150		
22																	S151		
23																	S152		
24																	S153		
25																	S154		
26																	S155		
27																	S156		
28																	S157		
29																	S158		

APPENDIX 3

EVALUATING THE CHURCH BULLETIN AND NEWSLETTER

The Bulletin

1. Does your bulletin include a regular place (not on an insert) that welcomes the visitors and tells them how to
   a. get information about Christianity;
   b. get information about Jesus Christ;
   c. find out how to join the church (this is not as important as items a and b)?

2. Is your bulletin easy to read with lots of white space?

3. Does your bulletin have an abundance of words or phrases that the unchurched might not know?

4. Is your bulletin designed more for a person who has never attended your church than for the members?

5. You can improve your bulletin using the following tips:
   a. Keep it simple and avoid clutter.
   b. Limit yourself to two fonts—one for headlines and one for the body. Avoid fonts that are hard to read, even if you like the way they look.
   c. Avoid using all capital letters. Using all capital letters to emphasize a point is like yelling. No one likes to be yelled at.
   d. Drastically limit the use of clip art and fancy borders.
   e. Keep column widths between two and four inches. Anything narrower or wider is difficult to read.
   f. Keep regular sections in the same places—especially the section that welcomes guests. Don't make readers hunt for what they need.
   g. Keep a file of well-designed bulletins to stimulate your ideas.

The Newsletter

1. Is it mailed at least monthly to everyone, including first-time visitors?
2. Can it be read in five minutes?
3. Is it free of poems or cute sayings?

APPENDIX 4

EVALUATING THE SITE, PROPERTY, AND FACILITIES

Accessibility

1. Does the church have any signs at various intersections pointing the way to the church? What do these signs tell you about the church? Are they neat and freshly painted? Are they obscured by brush or trees?

2. How easy is it to find the nursery, sanctuary, and the pastor's office without having to ask for directions?

3. Important property considerations:
   a. On how many acres does the church sit? How much of the land is usable? If your goal is to become a regional church, you need a minimum of eight acres, but thirty or more is better.
   b. How many sets of stairs does your church have? We are in a one-story world. The more stairs you have, the fewer people you will have at church in the twenty-first century. The country is getting older.
   c. How bright is the sanctuary? Bright is better than dim. It is hard to celebrate in a dark room.
   d. Is the location of the church visible to those passing by on major traffic arteries? Most churches are located five hundred feet off the beaten path.
   e. How wide are the halls? The minimum acceptable width is ten feet.

The Nursery

1. What is the appearance of the nursery? (How neat is it? Are things stored in the nursery that have nothing to do with infants? Is the carpet clean? Are the walls freshly painted? Are there windows?)

2. Is the nursery on the same floor as the sanctuary?

3. Is there a sign at every turn of the corridor showing the direction to the nursery and to the sanctuary?

4. Every room should have at least one paid worker. This person should be able to work with volunteers. This person should be regular in attendance so that the children see a familiar face when they arrive. You will have to pay this person well in order to ensure consistency.

5. Larger churches should employ a part-time person who oversees all of the nurseries, hires paid help, and recruits volunteers.

6. Require people to sign in when they leave children, even if the people are members of the church. It is best if you require them to leave their drivers' licenses when they leave their children. Do not allow a spouse to pick up the child; in today's world, it is impossible to know from week to week who is separated or divorced, and churches are becoming easy places in which to carry out noncustodial kidnapping.

7. Place a name tag on each child as he or she enters the room.

8. Give parents a pager or beeper that vibrates so that you can summon them if there is a problem. These instruments are not expensive anymore.

9. Give all first-time parents a brochure telling them about the nursery. Include such details as the procedures regarding dropping off and picking up children, how often you change the sheets and clean the toys, and so forth.

10. Give your nursery workers regular training.

11. Anytime the carpet has a stain that cannot be cleaned, replace the carpet, even if it is rather new.

12. Sanitize the room and toys after each use.

13. Keep the nurseries free of hazards. Do not allow parents to bring anything hot, such as coffee or tea, into the rooms. Do not stack things that toddlers could pull off on top of cabinets. Provide storage cabinets high enough that children cannot reach them. Most cleaning supplies should never be left in any nursery area.

14. Redecorate the entire nursery complex each year. Repaint and remove any damaged equipment, toys, or carpet.

15. Do not use the nursery for storage of any kind.

16. Use the nursery as an opportunity for evangelism:
    a. Take a picture of each first-time child and place it on the bulletin board. If the child does not return within three weeks, send the picture to the parents telling them you are still holding a place for their child.
    b. Send a letter of congratulation to the parents of all newborn children. If you have a large number of older adults, you may consider starting a "surrogate grandparent" ministry. Let new parents know about this ministry, in case they would like help rearing their child.
    c. Many churches ask new parents (members of their church) if they would like to have a lawn sign for a month that reads, "Newest member of (name of church)." The signs are either blue or pink and have a picture of a stork carrying a baby.

Construction Issues

For churches that are planning to build, the following is a suggested chronology to follow as you move into your building program.

1. Consultant planning.

2. Decision to move forward.

3. Building and program committee selection.

4. Selection and approval of architect.

5. Preliminary drawings.

6. Completed drawings.

During these preliminary stages, keep in mind the following steps toward improving your church's appearance:

a. Improve your curb appeal. The property needs to say "Welcome" to people passing by. It helps to create a point of interest that draws people's attention.

b. Create well-planned entrances to the property. Entrances should not be bottlenecks and should facilitate a safe and natural flow. They should not be more than six hundred feet from the parking lot.

c. Signs should be legible and perpendicular to the street. Drive by your church and clock the interval between when you can first read the sign and the time you pass it. The entire sign should be easily readable in that time period.

d. Develop a landscaped parking lot that provides one space for every two people at the time when the most people are on the proeprty. Reserve spaces for guests.

e. Provide security so that people will feel safe. Create an open feeling with no oversized bushes or hiding places. Good lighting is essential in the parking lot, entry way, and hallways.

f. Develop the site so that activity is clearly visible from the street. Playgrounds, parking lots, and major entrances should be visible to those passing by.

g. Maintain the facilities and grounds. Always keep the lawn mowed.

h. Concentrate on visitor-friendly touches, such as parking lot greeters and valets to assist elderly people and single parents with parking. Make sure welcome centers are highly visible.

i. Make sure the entrance to the sanctuary is large enough and has enough doors (usually two doors for every hundred people in worship. It is best if the lobby exits to the outside (rather than to an inside hallway, for example).

7. Building fund campaign.

8. Building fund celebration.

9. Completed bids.

10. Authorization of construction.

11. Ground breaking.

12. As you begin building, post a sign on the site telling the community what you are doing and when you plan to be finished.

13. Community outreach. When the facilities are completed, have an opening celebration and invite the community to attend. Send out invitations to all the families and individuals in the area asking them to join you for this great moment in the life of your church. Plan a way that those who do show up are encouraged to give you their names, addresses, and phone numbers, and then follow up on them. You will not have a big number of visitors, but the ones who do show up will be excellent potential new members or converts.

14. First Sunday celebration. Ask the Mayor (or another city official) to attend the celebration and take a small part.

15. Celebration year. Use the entire following year to celebrate this momentous event in the life of your church.

For churches that are thinking about building, the following questions and suggestions are intended to help you determine whether you need or are ready for a new facility.

1. What ministries will occur in this facility?

2. Will the people walk or drive to this facility?

3. What are the accessibility needs of this facility?
   a. What is the average age of the person using the facility now and forty years from now?
   b. Will we include ministries for those with mobility and hearing difficulties?

4. Will the number of people using this facility fluctuate throughout the year?

5. Is the entrance to the present facility large enough to ecourage people to enter and to fellowship?

6. Do the hallways in the present facility encourage conversation?

7. Is the nursery accessible?
   a. It should be on the same level as the sanctuary and as close to the sanctuary as possible.
   b. Is the area safe from someone entering from an outside door?
   c. Is there a dutch door separating the parents from the children?
   d. Is there separate space for "cribbers," "crawlers," and "walkers"?
   e. Are there thirty square feet per child in each of the areas?
   f. Is there a sink and changing table in each room?
   g. Can the nursery be restricted to nursery use only?

8. The following questions apply to the sanctuary.

a. Is the seating based on twenty-two to twenty-four inches per person?
b. Is there a parking space for every two people?
c. Can the entrance be seen from the street?
d. Is the sanctuary set back from the street corner, and does the parking area wrap around the sanctuary?
e. Is at least a portion of the parking area visible from the street and not entirely hidden by the sanctuary.
f. If the sanctuary is used three or more times on Sunday morning, is the sanctuary's capacity twice as large as the educational facility's capacity?
g. Can the sanctuary be used while Sunday school is taking place?
h. Do the exits encourage everyone to exit into a large lobby that is also a fellowship area?
i. Is there a place in the lobby for a book table or bookstore?
j. Will the sanctuary be designed primarily for preaching or for the administration of the sacraments?
k. Has the use of visual media been taken into consideration?
l. Is there a good sound system and are there enough electrical outlets?
m. Is there room on stage for drama presentations and an orchestra?
n. What role do we want the choir or choirs to play?
o. What will this sanctuary look like when it is half full?
p. Can additions be made to this sanctuary in the future without it looking as if it has been altered?
q. Is there a registration area in the lobby?
r. Have parking spaces for visitors been considered?
s. Have parking spaces for single parents been considered?
t. Will the people we are targeting prefer pews or padded theater seats?
u. Are the pews too long?
v. Is there an entrance to the sanctuary within six hunded feet of the most distant space in the parking lot?
w. Is the pastor's office accessible from both the inside and the outside of the building?

9. The following questions apply to educational facilities.
   a. Is everyone aware that educational facilities never pay for themselves?
   b. Have we considered two sessions of Sunday school or alternate sites for classes or small groups augmenting Sunday school?
   c. Are the classrooms designed to be attractive meeting rooms first and classrooms second?
   d. Is each room going to be without sound overflow from other rooms?
   e. Have we taken into account that multimedia presentations will be essential in the twenty-first century?
   f. Will the first unit include one large room that can be used as a large lecture class led by the pastor?
   g. Is the lighting bright and cheerful?
   h. Do the classrooms vary in size?

10. The following questions apply to the office area.
   a. Is the office a self-contained unit in terms of heating, cooling, security, and restrooms?

b. Is the staff space designed for growth?

c. Does the staff space have its own private conference room?

d. Is the area designed for computer networking?

e. Is there a large space where office volunteers can work during the week?

f. Have you spent disproportionately more on the office area than on the nursery, parking lot, or parlor?

g. Has some member who is knowledgeable about business environments looked over the plans for the office?

h. Has "flow" (the office traffic pattern) been considered?

11. What will be the first impression on the people passing by?

a. Is the primary sign readable to people who pass by?

b. Have we considered using flower beds for color?

c. Does a person standing in the parking lot know where to go to find the sanctuary or a place for information?

12. Have we considered the appropriate number of restrooms, and do they include changing areas for infants?

13. Is there a room for choir rehearsal where the choir cannot be heard in the sanctuary?

14. Have energy costs been considered?

15. Have we installed air-conditioning so that we can be a twelve-month church?

For congregations who are ready to select a new size for a church, asking the following questions about the sites you are considering should help you make the right choice.

1. Is there drainage and storm water control?

2. What are the subsoil conditions?

3. Is there access to public utilities?

4. Are we considering enough acres?

5. Are their any goverment restrictions against churches building on this property?

6. Is this property accessible?

7. Is this property highly visible?

8. What are the future plans of the city for the streets in this area?

For churches who are ready to choose an architect, the following questions are intended to help you evaluate your candidates.

1. Does this person exibit creativity in design and process?

2. How flexible is this person? Will he or she work with us to build what we want, or will he or she build what he or she wants?

3. Would this be someone we would want to work with in the future?

4. What is the integrity of this person's earlier projects—both structurally and functionally?

5. How accurate have this person's estimates been on recent projects?

6. Does this person have access to computer software that will allow you to see three-dimensional pictures of his or her designs?

7. How good is this person in executing his or her designs?

8. Is this person capable of meeting your deadlines?

9. Will this person be the principal person working on your project, or will a junior person be responsible?

10. Is this person able to work with other consultants or is he or she a loner?

11. Does this person have access to other good, sound architects or consultants?

12. Are this person and the person from the church assigned to supervise this project compatible?

13. What is this person's fee structure?